'As with all his writings, David Runco
a warmth of human empathy that ena
opinions and experiences to enter into ~ ~~~~~~ engagement
with Scripture. This is a book full of insights and its publication
is timely.'
Robert Atwell, Bishop of Exeter

'The Bible speaks of God's faithful love for everyone. David
unfolds this truth to a conflicted Church, and to a world in
desperate need of that good news. *Love Means Love* is brim-full
of gentle and clear wisdom. Highly recommended!'
Paul Bayes, Bishop of Liverpool

'Joyful, truthful, scandalously inclusive . . . at times I could
hardly read it for sheer joy. This book will literally save lives. It
opens the door of grace and beckons you in.'
Nick Bundock, Rector, St James and Emmanuel, Didsbury

'Offers particularly fine insights . . . deeply orthodox and will
also give plenty of food for thought to those who think that to
be pro-LGBTQ+ is perforce to have to abandon Scripture. One
of the best short books on the subject I've read.'
Simon Butler, parish priest and member of the Archbishops'
Council

'David Runcorn writes to encourage acceptance of faithful
same-sex relationships. He does so with a deep respect for both
the teaching of the Bible and the lived experience of LGBTQ+
people who have often felt excluded by the Church. Both gracious and scholarly, with the pastoral touch that shows sound
understanding of the science of humanity and sexuality, this

book puts the gospel of God's love at the heart of our message to the nation. Heartily recommended!'
David Gillett, Bishop of Bolton (1999–2008)

'David Runcorn offers that rare gift – perspective. Through each of his short chapters, David demonstrates an understanding of the changing ways in which the Christian community has talked about LGBTQ+ people over recent decades. Ideas often presented as "biblical" are questioned, placed in their developing cultural context, and David finds instead a greater grace on every page – a vision of a Church and a world where love means love.'
Marcus Green, author of *The Possibility of Difference: A biblical affirmation of inclusivity*

'A gentle and insightful book, written with humility, which will greatly help those seeking an informed understanding of key biblical texts with an open mind. David's thoughts on how we read in an age of anxiety are particularly perceptive. I heartily recommend this work to anyone wishing to engage carefully with the topic.'
Nikki Groarke, Archdeacon, Dudley, and member of the Church of England's General Synod

'Warm, reflective, surprising, challenging, scriptural, human and focused on Jesus, this is a different kind of book . . . Writing with a compassion and spiritual depth that encompasses a breadth of human experience, David Runcorn engages with key texts and traditional views, and comes to very positive and scripturally based conclusions about God's gift of sexuality.'
David Ison, Dean, St Paul's, London

David Runcorn is a speaker, writer, teacher and trainer, working in areas of personal vocational guidance, spiritual direction, prayer, Christian faith and theology. His books circle around the connecting themes between all these topics and are a continuing exploration of what faith and human flourishing mean in a world like ours.

David is ordained in the Church of England and has been a vicar in London, a leader and community member of a large conference and holiday centre in North Devon, a theological college teacher, diocesan Director of Ministry and, most recently, a Director of Ordinands and Warden of Readers in the Diocese of Gloucester.

He lives in Devon.

LOVE MEANS LOVE

Same-sex relationships and the Bible

David Runcorn

British Library Cataloguing-in-Publication Data
A catalogue record for this book is available from the British Library

ISBN 978-0-281-08441-8
eBook ISBN 978-0-281-08442-5

1 3 5 7 9 10 8 6 4 2

Typeset by Manila Typesetting Company
First printed in Great Britain by Ashford Colour Press
Subsequently digitally reprinted in Great Britain

eBook by Manila Typesetting Company

Produced on paper from sustainable forests

Contents

Acknowledgements

I am grateful to a large number of people, representing a variety of views and convictions, who have read all or parts of this book, engaged elsewhere with these themes and offered generous and honest feedback. They include especially Simon, John, Angela, Ali, Bishop David G., Simon, Robert, Bishop David A., Penny, Richard, Bishop Michael, Tudor, Simon, Susannah, Andy, George, Erika and David. Special thanks once again to my dear wife Jackie for her patience and encouragement, living with a husband in obsessive writing mode. Simon Kingston, once again, has been a significant critical friend to the emerging text.

My thanks also to Alison Barr and the publishing team at SPCK for their belief in this project and for enthusiastically bringing it to print.

I want to make special mention of my mentor and dear friend Roger Hurding, who died while this book was in the writing. Its theme was close to his heart. Over the years, despite the confines of long-term severe ill health, his influence as a friend, counsellor and pastoral theologian was profound. He engaged widely and generously on web discussion forums, in personal correspondence and conversation. Roger helped many people to explore an informed shape to their faith and beliefs during times when spaces for trusting and open discussion were not easy to find. His unfailingly gracious tone helped to sustain conversations through strong disagreement. Along with many others, I acknowledge my grateful debt to him over the years.

Through his words and presence, many came to a transforming appreciation of the wideness of God's love. My prayer is that something of his spirit is found in this book.

Love Means Love is published as the Church of England prepares to initiate an extended discussion and teaching programme on identity, relationships and sexuality called 'Living in Love and Faith' (www.churchofengland.org/LLF). *Love Means Love* is the fruit of a personal journey with the Bible offered to all who are seeking to explore our often conflicted understanding of human being and becoming.

1

On opening doors: introducing the discussion

This book is written for Christians seeking to understand and live the call of Christ to love one another; and within that calling it is particularly offered for anyone interested in thinking through what Christians believe about the Bible, sex and same-sex relationships.

We, the community of people reading this book, are seeking to work out life and faith in a Church that continues to be deeply divided over what it believes about homosexuality. We are a very varied community. Some of us are gay. Some of us are civil-partnered or married. Some of us are straight. Some of us live on our own, some of us in couples, in intentional communities or in families of all shapes and sizes.

What I assume we have in common, because you have picked up this book, is this: that we want to know what the Bible has to say about human sexuality and, in particular, to understand how the Bible teaches and guides us about same-sex relationships. This subject has become one of the most preoccupying and conflicted issues of our times.

Many of us find ourselves living with a dilemma. We are Christians for whom the Bible is read and reverenced as the guiding authority for life and faith. On the particular issue of sexuality, however, we struggle with, or are no longer able to accept, traditional understandings of what the Bible teaches on same-sex relationships. This is an uncomfortable place to be.

We can feel dishonest as we quietly dissent from the apparent 'plain meaning' of certain parts of the Bible or from the convictions we hear preached in church or from views expressed in our own communities. It is hard to gauge our numbers for we have often struggled to know how to bring our voices and questions to this highly conflicted debate. My own experience suggests that we are a significant and growing group.[1]

We are vulnerably aware that our questions present an unsettling challenge to the way the Bible has long been read and understood on this subject. We find it unsettling too. After all, those who believe that the Bible is clear in condemning same-sex relationships have a long history on their side. They can also appeal to what seems to be the 'plain meaning' of the texts. However, these familiar readings are being increasingly challenged. One effect of this is that our questions here extend beyond one particular issue: we are confronted with how we read the Bible at all.

Another challenge we face is that, by opening up this discussion, our fellowship with one another is tested. In having come to believe, as I do, that love means love and that committed same-sex expressions of love may be blessed and good in God's eyes, I am painfully aware that some of my dearest friends hold a different view.

Some of us belong to churches that believe the Bible forbids same-sex relationships and are very upfront in declaring this. Questions on this issue are not welcome. It takes a certain courage to even raise them in such contexts, especially if we do not feel trained or equipped to do so. For lack of somewhere to explore our questions with others, many of us stay silent, privately dissenting from the prevailing view in communities we call our spiritual home. Some have left churches over this issue; some have been asked to leave.

Across all the traditions there are many other churches that have never expressed a particular view on sexuality but where open and informed discussion has yet to happen. It is a painfully divisive issue. Church leaders and their communities can be tempted to avoid the subject for fear of the conflict it causes, but this silence serves no one well. I have heard too many stories, for example, of parents with a child who is gay or folk who are themselves gay, simply unable to share something so central to their lives with fellow church members for fear of what the reaction would be. Silence also means that people are not being enabled to grow in faith and confidence, to develop an informed understanding of the Scriptures or to read and interpret them. Silence does not communicate nothing. It can and does result in a steady loss of confidence in the Bible as a source of truth, guidance and wisdom.

There are among us those whose personal journeys of faith and identity have left their relationship with the Bible badly damaged. Quite simply, some of us have not found our own story told, loved or understood there and have been left feeling judged and unwelcome. In the absence of being shown any other way of reading and understanding the Scriptures, some have finally given up on them altogether.

We need to open up this discussion without anxiety. We need to learn how to love without fear as we explore new patterns of relating and belonging. We have not been here before. There are still too few open, exploratory places where Bibles can be studied, difficult questions asked, understanding tested out, wounds healed and differences faced respectfully. There are examples of local support and training events designed to help church communities understand what 'welcome' actually means in this context, but more are needed. 'Welcome' is so much more than a word on the church noticeboard or weekly notice sheet.[2]

We find ourselves on this journey of faith and belief for a variety of reasons. If we express a progressive understanding of same-sex relationships, it is often assumed that we must have changed our minds at some point. Not all of us have. Some, like me, have never been convinced by the way the Bible has been interpreted and taught on this subject. But seeking the theological and biblical resources with which to test out our questions has not been easy. An informed understanding takes time. Theology has followed our questions, as it sometimes must.

Others have changed their beliefs. Often it has been the impact of knowing friends, colleagues or loved ones who are gay. We are simply unable to recognize them, their faith, their goodness or their relationships in the biblical text, which appears only to judge and condemn. A father spoke of the impact on him when his teenage son told him he was gay. He was a teacher of theology who had already given the subject a lot of thought, but now:

> the traditionalist treatment of sexual orientation seemed shallow and unhelpful to my wife and me when we looked at our son. [His] resolute good humour and goodwill, his natural abilities and easy-going nature all seemed clearly and self-evidently to say 'there is nothing wrong here!' Or to put it a bit more precisely, we considered him normal and healthy, someone in need of the grace of God, as we all are, but not deeply troubled.[3]

The case from the Bible for the affirmation and full inclusion of homosexual men and women and of committed same-sex relationships is a cumulative one. It is not based on one text. So this book is perhaps like a map: it traces the paths through the Scriptures that lead, I believe, to new understanding through fresh approaches to interpretation. My hope is that the book will help to clarify how folks like me have come to these convictions. I also hope it may be a resource for individuals and Christian communities who are seeking to work out their own understanding of homosexuality and same-sex relationships from the Scriptures.

Two concerns often surface in discussions on this subject. The first is: will I be abandoning the Bible if I support same-sex relationships? The conviction of this book is that supporting same-sex relationships does not involve any contradiction or denial of what the Bible teaches. The issue, as it always is, is how the Bible is interpreted. In the following chapters I offer examples of how the Bible can be read as supporting faithful same-sex relationships without bypassing the 'awkward' passages. I believe it is possible to read the Bible with integrity and in obedience, in such a way as to speak welcome instead of condemnation.

The second concern is: will I be condoning promiscuity if I support gay relationships? The answer again is no. We might wonder where this question comes from. After all, sexual infidelity and relational fragility are endemic within heterosexual communities, but no one claims that supporting heterosexual relationships means condoning promiscuity. In Chapter 4, I shall explore the influence of the personal stories we bring to this debate. For many of us, negative assumptions about homosexuality and same-sex relating have been formed through powerful social conditioning, often from our very early years. This has been particularly true for men. Translations and interpretations of the Scriptures have played their part too. I examine and challenge these. For example, the story of Sodom and readings of the first chapters of the letter to the Romans have been significant in giving same-sex relationships an extreme notoriety in the popular Christian imagination. While the actual lives and faith of gay people remained hidden from local church communities, much of what was assumed about them and their relationships was easily based on ignorance, prejudice, poor Bible interpretation and biased reporting. The result too often was a pitiless exclusion and actual violence for which both the Church and society have been notoriously slow to acknowledge their responsibility.

This is changing. The more visible presence, participation and evidently fruitful lives of gay people in the Church and society have been challenging stereotypes and re-informing opinion. Discussions are now based on the principle of talking *with*, not *about* – though old habits die hard. This needs time because the wounds are deep and the stories raw, but it also means that the reading and interpreting of Scripture are now taking place *with*, and not at a theoretical distance *from*, those whose lives and relationships are actually being discussed.

It should not really need saying that those in committed same-sex relationships aspire to the same Christian standards of loving faithfulness and holiness of life as those in heterosexual relationships. For too long they have had to work out their love burdened by the need for secrecy, in isolation and in the face of actual opposition, without any of the social, spiritual and relational support that all relationships need in order to flourish and endure. If fragility is apparent here, it is surely not surprising. But there is also so much to admire. The Archbishop of Canterbury has spoken of the 'stunning relationships' of some known to him.[4]

There is a memorable moment in J. R. R. Tolkien's *The Lord of the Rings* trilogy. The company have travelled long enough to know that their mission is fraught with hidden dangers and violent opposition. Their world, until recently benignly peaceable, is now a hostile place. Their journey has brought them reluctantly to the entrance of ancient mines under the mountains, the huge old doors to which are shut fast. Light is fading and the mood threatening. They are weary and anxious. This is not a place to linger. Above the doors are engraved the words 'Speak friend and enter'. They assume that a password is needed and try every word they can think of but to no avail. Suddenly, one of them laughs aloud, realizing that the message was written in friendlier times and meant exactly what it said. Standing in front of the entrance, he says 'Friend', and the doors open wide to allow them to enter.[5]

Speaking in friendship in strange and threatening contexts is not the most natural or wise response. Historically, homosexuality has been seen as the enemy of all that is godly and good. Our debates often come up against firmly closed doors. There is no magic password on offer. The invitation is to speak in faithful love and friendship. As we do, we pray that what is closed will begin to open to a community seeking to move forwards in the call to love one another and bear fresh witness to ways of living and belonging together.

2

'That my house may be filled': Jesus and the new community

An air of astonishment surrounds the earthly ministry of Jesus. Wherever he went his words and actions awakened wonder, shock, joy, bewilderment and scandal in equal measure. The most unsettling surprise was the revelation of who was welcomed and given a place at the table in the new community of Jesus, for familiar social, moral and religious boundaries were ignored. The most unlikely people were found there, including those usually excluded from that conservatively religious society – the poor, disabled, victimized and sick, and penitent outsiders. Meanwhile, those who most expected to be there were often not included.

The religious 'good', with their impeccable, hard-won reputations and scrupulous scriptural fidelity, were constantly scandalized by Jesus. He broke the rules and reread the texts. He ignored their reputations and bypassed expected measures of goodness, respectability and holiness, ministering to and mixing with the 'wrong' sorts of people and even eating in their homes. Jesus in particular confronted religious devotion which had become a self-interested piety that was loveless, judgmental and excluding of others. Nothing made him angrier. He pointed instead to the excluded, marginalized, undeserving and irreligious joyfully entering and finding home in God's love. Look, he said, 'the tax-collectors and the prostitutes are going into the kingdom of God ahead of you'

(Matthew 21.31). Whenever Jesus wanted to illustrate the life of the kingdom, he spoke of abundance, feasting and celebration. If those religious insiders who had long had an invitation on their mantelpiece chose to stay away, the doors were opened even wider to any and all beyond, 'that my house may be filled' (Luke 14.23). The church of Christ in every time and place will always be found working out the shock and surprise of God's unfolding ways.

In the Jewish tradition, to be a disciple of a rabbi meant not only following his commands and teachings but also living and acting *exactly* as he did. So what kind of community can we expect to emerge where the words and actions of Jesus are imitated? The answer is one marked by unconditional welcome, abundant hospitality (given and received), mercy where only judgement was expected, loving touch without regard for taint and reputation and, above all, a scandalous, generous inclusion. This is as true today as it was in Jesus' time.

The first churches struggled with the challenge presented by such a community. In particular, theological and cultural divisions between Jewish and Gentile believers can be found running like an unresolved fault-line through the whole New Testament era. This was their equivalent of our present-day conflicts over sexuality.

In Chapter 8, I suggest this as a way of understanding Paul's letter to the Roman church. After long and careful teaching, which forms the theological heart of the New Testament, Paul turns, in the last few chapters, to offer pastoral guidelines for a conflicted church. We know it was a very diverse community – ethnically, theologically, culturally and in its divisions between Jews and Gentiles, rich and poor. Among the Jewish Christians were an influential group of traditionalists who believed it was essential to continue to observe Jewish customs in its life and worship – circumcision, food laws, Jewish calendar, festivals and the sabbath. This is quite probably the group whose self-righteous judgementalism Paul confronts in Romans chapter 2. By contrast, Gentile believers had come to faith without meeting any of those demands; they believed that they lived by grace and were not required to keep the Jewish law and practices. Surely they were free of such obligations? Conservative believers and those holding more progressive beliefs were thus living awkwardly together in one community. That sounds very familiar to readers in today's Church.

This was not a minor matter of accommodating group preferences. At issue was the whole identity of the Church and its mission. So how did Paul respond? Strikingly, he does not approach the conflict in terms of right or wrong belief, though he has his own views on this, as he teaches elsewhere. He is more concerned to lay down the basis for shared life in a community with significant differences – what we might call 'good disagreeing'. Paul is not saying that truth does not matter or is just a matter of private opinion. The deepening of scriptural faith and understanding remains of central importance to him, as it should for us.

Paul's starting point is to insist that they genuinely accept one another as brothers and sisters in Christ. The basis for meeting as the body of Christ is always a mutual tolerance. So, while they may be deeply concerned about the keeping of food and dietary laws, the Jewish traditionalist group is not to judge or exclude Gentile believers who do not see that as an issue of faith. 'Those who eat must not despise those who abstain, and those who abstain must not pass judgement on those who eat; for God has welcomed them' (Romans 14.3). Likewise, those proclaiming their freedom from such rules must not look down on 'weaker'

11

conservatives and their observances as though from some superior place of faith. 'Exclusivism is the besetting sin of religious conservatives [and] smugness of the besetting sin of religious liberals.'[1] Addressing both groups, Paul says:

> Let all be fully convinced in their own minds. . . . [Let] those who eat, eat in honour of the LORD, since they give thanks to God; while those who abstain, abstain in honour of the LORD and give thanks to God. We do not live to ourselves, and we do not die to ourselves. If we live, we live to the LORD, and if we die, we die to the LORD; so then, whether we live or whether we die, we are the LORD's. (Romans 14.5–8)

The priority for Paul, in a church where strongly conflicting views are sincerely held, is that all of us are living 'for/of/to the LORD'. The phrase occurs a number of times in these chapters (Romans 14.4, 6, 8) and in his other letters. Chris Marshall summarizes Paul's position:

> If another holds a view that you disagree with, perhaps passionately, and that you may even consider to be a totally inappropriate belief for a Christian to hold, as long as that person has come to his or her views in conscious submission to the teaching of Christ, and holds it with a clear conscience, in thankfulness to God and aware of the coming Day when he/she will give account of themselves to God, then you are duty bound to welcome that sister or brother in the same way that Christ has welcomed you.[2]

Here are helpful biblical principles for living faithfully in a divided church. We need them today as the people of God struggle once again with issues of boundaries, welcome and inclusion in the church of Christ. When it comes to the presence of believers in the Church who happen to be gay, the language of welcome and inclusion is often used in a misleading way. The welcome we are speaking of here is not the belated goodwill of a church that has held traditional views but has now decided to 'include' those whom it previously opposed and excluded. It is Christ who welcomes. It is Christ who includes. We are the church of Christ. The Church itself is not the centre of the story and never has been. This is illustrated in Chapter 12, where I explore the story of Peter and Cornelius (Acts chapter 10). That story of shockingly radical welcome and inclusion transformed the Christian Church from being a narrow Jewish sect into a faith for all peoples. It did not come about as a result of Jewish Christians welcoming and including Gentiles. Quite the reverse. Peter and the Jewish believers in Jerusalem had to realize that they were not the centre of God's surprising activity at all. It was Peter who had to journey to and cross a threshold into a world that he had believed was forbidden to him. There he received, as a surprising gift, *his own* inclusion and welcome in a story already revealed by the Spirit in the life and faith of an outsider. Jews and Gentiles were actually on a journey together, beyond their own understanding, preferred boundaries and limited expectations, into the welcome of the new community of Christ. I find that a helpful illustration of the shared journeys required in today's Church.

Now, as then, the life and mission of the Church is not for understanding in the sense of one group calling another to its viewpoint as if one were right and the other wrong. Both need the courage and faithfulness to go *'to a place that neither has ever been before'*.[3] I believe that this is the challenge we face with the issue of sexuality and the relationships of faithful fellow believers.

Through the pages of this book, I have sought to explain how, from Scripture, tradition and in the guiding presence of Christ, I believe our calling is to become communities in which all women and men journey together into the wide, including welcome of the kingdom of God.

3

The surprise of God?
Dialogue with and beyond the word

On 6 September 1620, a boat called the *Mayflower* set sail from
Plymouth in England for North America. Among those on
board were Puritan pilgrims seeking a new home and freedom
for their Nonconformist faith and practices. They had endured
sustained persecution in England, including harassment, con-
fiscation of property and imprisonment. One group had travelled from the Netherlands where they were already in exile.
Before they left, a pastor called John Robinson preached these
words to them on the dockside:

> 'I charge you before God . . . that you follow me no further
> than you have seen me follow the Lord Jesus Christ. If God
> reveals anything to you by any other instrument of His,
> be as ready to receive it as you were to receive any truth by
> my ministry, for I am verily persuaded the Lord hath more
> truth yet to break forth out of His Holy Word.' He went on
> to lament how Lutheran and Calvinist groups of their day
> were clinging to their own tribal allegiances. He believed
> that it left them closed to precisely the renewing faith God
> was calling those pilgrims to.[1]

There is an impressive courage and hopefulness in his words,
given their experience of marginalization and suffering.
Oppressed groups can easily close in on themselves to protect

what is distinctive about their identity and beliefs. Robinson calls them to be open and trusting in the face of the unknown. There is always more to be revealed: Christian faith is outward-looking.

What Robinson said about 'His Holy Word' is much loved and oft quoted within the Evangelical tradition. 'To break forth' suggests a dynamic energy at work that will not be confined or hemmed in. 'Yet' – there is always newness to be revealed out of what is already given. So the relationship of the faithful to the Scriptures is to be always open and trusting. Our understanding is never exhausted and in every time and place more will be breaking forth to guide the people of God in the challenges and questions they are facing.

Oliver O'Donovan shares Robinson's openness but expresses it even more boldly: 'We have to be alert to the possibility . . . of doctrine being renewed out of Scripture in a way that takes the church by surprise.'[2]

Are there any limits to where this newness might lead? And if it really is new, how will we recognize it? There are those who argue nothing can be accepted that goes beyond what Scripture already teaches, that the Bible sets a firm boundary around the development of further understanding. In which case, nothing is actually new. There is only the task of *renewing* or rediscovering what was already in the text – always supposing we have rightly understood it in the first place.

This approach is often accompanied by a belief that the Bible speaks with one voice and one core meaning and teaching runs through it all. Nothing can go beyond it and nothing more is actually needed. Seeking the will of God on any issue or question is a matter of reading the relevant Scriptures and obeying them. In that way we will surely come to the correct answer on all major questions of ethics. So, if, for example, the Bible only ever condemns same-sex sexual activity and there are no positive examples of any faithful same-sex relationships, how can homosexuality claim to be 'biblical'?

In his book *Having Words with God: The Bible as conversation*, Karl Allen Kuhn challenges this:

> Scripture itself provides no indication that the dynamic nature of God's instruction is suddenly to cease. To insist, as some do, that all of the specific injunctions of the New Testament concerning particular behaviours must stand for all time *is to assign to biblical instruction a role that it has never before performed.*[3]

Kuhn points out just how much of the Bible is a dialogue rather than a 'monological', prescriptive text. God is constantly in conversation with his people and they with him. The Bible texts and writers are also in dialogue with one another. It is notable, for example, that with very few exceptions the New Testament writers (and Jesus himself) never quote or allude to Old Testament texts without adapting or modifying them, literally and/or theologically.[4] A continual theological dialogue is going on through which new understanding is explored. That there are four Gospel accounts (and extended discussions by letters) means that even Jesus' own ministry and teaching is not captured in one clear text. 'It is not only the words of Scripture that matter (and they matter very much). The dynamic, ongoing sacred dialogue that Scripture reflects and calls believers to take part in is equally essential to biblical faith.'[5]

One example is of some relevance to our discussion. It is the recurring issue of racial separation, purity and intermarriage in the Bible. There are several passages where God commands the total ethnic cleansing of non-Israelites in the promised land (Deuteronomy 7 and 20; Joshua 11.16–23). The people Moses originally led out of Egypt, however, included a mixture of races (Exodus 12.38) and Moses himself was married to a Midianite woman. Much later, when the Israelites returned from exile to rebuild Jerusalem, their leader Nehemiah insisted that all married couples of mixed race must separate: 'Thus I cleansed them from everything foreign' (Nehemiah 13.30). In another place, the prophet Isaiah teaches: 'Do not let the foreigner joined to the LORD say, "The LORD will surely separate me from his people" . . . For thus says the LORD: . . . I will give [them] a name better than sons and daughters' (Isaiah 56.3, 4, 5). Meanwhile, the book of Ruth, named after a Moabite woman, not only celebrates a mixed-race marriage but Ruth, the outsider, also becomes the great-grandmother of King David. This means that discerning 'what the Bible says' on purity and inclusion involves careful listening to a variety of contexts and to the way in which parts of the Bible speak to, challenge and even appear to contradict one another. Nowhere are these tensions resolved and gathered into one message. While the New Testament vision of the Church moves beyond racial boundaries altogether, it remains a deeply divisive issue within the first churches, as witnessed by the continuing struggles between Jewish and Gentile believers (see Ephesians 2.11–22 for an example of Paul's response to this conflict).

The subject of slavery also offers an example of dialogue both within and *beyond* the Bible. No Christian today believes slavery to be anything other than a godless evil. Nowhere does the Bible actually say that, however. There are no texts that explicitly condemn slavery, and through Christian history it has been worryingly easy to believe the opposite. The nineteenth-century abolitionists had no Scripture texts on which they could base their claim that slavery was contrary to the will of God. They were mocked for being 'revisionists'.

Even within the Bible, the subject of slavery is complex and the work of interpretation is not straightforward. In the book of Exodus, those who kidnapped and sold people were condemned to death (21.16), but was this ruling limited to the kidnapping and selling of Hebrew slaves? If so, was the trafficking of foreigners permitted? Though the text is not clear, that is certainly how businesses justified recruiting for the cotton fields of the West Indies and Southern states of America. There are Bible texts that regulate slave-keeping and others seem to be aimed at limiting exploitation, but nowhere is it actually prohibited. Even the New Testament accepts slavery without protest. We also bring our own assumptions as twenty-first-century Christians to the debate. Slavery, as commonly imagined, is abject servitude, but in some of Jesus' parables slaves were powerful business managers (Luke 16.1–8). When we read that Christ became a slave for us and that we are to imitate him (Philippians 2.5–8), what kind of slavery is in mind? And is this based on the ancient world of the Bible or on reflections from Roman society at the time?

The claim that slavery is evil and against the will of God goes beyond what the Scripture texts actually teach anywhere. When we take such a view today and call it 'biblical', we are insisting that particular Bible texts need to be understood within the broader scriptural principles of God's compassion and justice, through the words and actions of Jesus and much more. The same interpretive method is needed to inform our discussions about sexuality and relationships.

The slavery debate also highlights how Bible translations can mislead. English translations unhelpfully use the word 'slavery' to translate a variety of Hebrew words that themselves reveal a range of different kinds of employment or ownership practices in ancient Israel. With the concept reduced to one word, a whole world of more varied meanings and practices is lost or simply misinterpreted.

A dialogical approach has always been the way in which the Church has sought a faithful and discerning reading of Scripture – even among those who might be expected to resist the idea. Evangelical history reveals a tradition uncompromisingly committed to obeying the Bible as Christians' unique authority and guide. It has been willing, though often fiercely reactive at first, to revise, reverse, accept and include new understandings of social and ethical issues it previously opposed on the grounds of Scripture. The list would include slavery, apartheid, usury, divorce and remarriage, the death penalty, contraception, and women in society and in the church. The unsettling process of reading, re-examining, repenting, reinterpreting and revising even long unquestioned biblical convictions under the compelling of the Spirit, and in the light of contemporary questions, is not a task this tradition is unfamiliar with or unwilling to undertake. Indeed its own understanding of Scripture requires it.

The dialogical approach offers ways to address the question of how to read the Scriptures for wisdom about issues or people it (1) originally addressed in more than one way and in very different contexts; (2) does not directly address at all; or (3) would not even recognize or understand, within its own world – the issue we are faced with today.

The theologian Tom Wright likens the relationship of the Church to Scripture as a participation in a five-act play.[6] The first four acts are the creation, the Fall, Israel and Jesus. The first scene of act five is the New Testament. The continuing life of the Church in act five is not simply a verbatim repetition of that first scene. Rather it offers a dynamic improvisation. As every actor knows, to improvise faithfully requires a deep, obedient and sustained immersion in the first four acts. No one is making anything up. But this does challenge approaches to Scripture that assume a single, controlling interpretation of the text that can then be simply applied to our own context. This provides the basis for O'Donovan's surprises and Robinson's expectation of 'yet more'.

Down through history the Church, with its Bible open, has struggled with and then accepted (with varying degrees of graciousness and intelligence) the emerging insights of cosmology, evolution, biology, social sciences, medical research and much else. This has consistently required reconsideration of what kind of revelation the Bible actually is, the nature of its authority and how it speaks to the fresh challenges and experiences each generation encounters. This process has not been without attempts to stay in biblical bubbles – such as the Catholic Church's treatment of Galileo, or the Victorian naturalist Philip Gosse's refusal to believe the visible evidence of evolutionary processes because he believed the Bible taught that God made the world complete, in a moment, but with all the appearance of age, such as rock strata, tree rings and even a navel for Adam.[7]

In his book *Beyond the Bible: Moving from Scripture to theology*, the Evangelical theologian Howard Marshall argues that living, obedient faith always requires the willingness to go beyond the Bible text. He admits there are risks involved in this, but he is clear as to which risk he thinks is the greater: that of being misled by reading the Bible only in a first-century (or earlier) time warp and refusing to go beyond the letter of Scripture: 'We must be aware of the danger of failing to understand what God is saying to his people today and muzzling his voice. Scripture itself constrains us to the task of on-going theological development.'[8]

The Anglican Church's relationship to Scripture has been summarized in this way:

> Anglicans affirm the sovereign authority of the Holy Scriptures as the medium through which God by the Spirit communicates his word in the Church. The Scriptures are the uniquely inspired witness to divine revelation, and the primary norm for Christian faith and life. The Scriptures must be translated, read and understood, and their meaning grasped through a continuing process of interpretation.[9]

Notice this statement is in the present tense. This is about a living, dynamic revelation that we encounter now. Notice too that Scripture is a unique witness to a divine revelation: *it is not the revelation itself.* The Spirit communicates through God's word to the church. We in our turn have the task of seeking its meaning through reading, understanding and 'a continuing process of interpretation'. Interpretation is the way through which we seek to understand the meaning and therefore authority of the text, and begin to discern what responses of life and faith are being asked of our context and time.

Here is the challenge I think we are facing. The church has found, in its midst, a significant and increasingly visible community of people. They are disciples of Christ, living in obedience to word and spirit, faithful witnesses and gifts to those among whom they live. They seek only to live in committed sacrificial love to the one they believe to be God's gift to them. Despite all this, they do not find their particular stories of pilgrimage, faith and love told anywhere in the Bible. They are simply absent from the texts. Nor do they recognize themselves in the ways the Church has long spoken of them. They happen to be gay.

If the Church is to embrace the challenges and receive the newness this brings, it requires, in the first instance, the willingness to be taken by surprise.

4

The Bible in an age of anxiety: worry, reality and trust

'Do not worry,' Jesus told his followers in the Sermon on the Mount (Matthew 6.25–34). What does worrying actually achieve? he asks. It is of no practical use. 'Do not worry about anything,' wrote Paul to Christians who were living in very vulnerable and uncertain circumstances. Instead they were to offer all to God and to live in prayerful trust: 'The LORD is near' (Philippians 4.6, 5).

Christians are called to be a non-anxious presence in the world – as God is non-anxious. This is not because there is nothing to care deeply about, to be concerned for or to speak out about. There are – but we are to do it from a place of trust, not out of anxiety, worry and fear.

Anxiety is a major feature in society today. Mental health organizations report that 20–30 per cent of the population at any one time are struggling with anxiety-related conditions.[1] The rabbi, psychotherapist and social theorist Edwin Freidman wrote that chronic anxiety has become the driver in much of Western society. By that he meant something far more pervasive than a tendency to be over-concerned about things. The anxiety he had in mind

> may be compared to the volatile atmosphere of a room filled with gas fumes, where any sparking incident could set off a conflagration and where people would then blame the person who struck the match rather than trying to disperse

the fumes. The issues over which anxious systems become concerned, therefore, are more likely to be the focus of anxiety rather than its cause.[2]

Anxiety is never far from the surface in the Church now facing immense challenges to its life and existence. There is the struggle to be an effective presence in a society largely adrift from any rooted beliefs. There are the challenges to grow and to reverse long-term decline. Within its own life the Church of England's journey towards the full partnership of women and men in ministry and leadership has been long and exhausting and is still conflicted. The debate over sexuality and same-sex relationships is the latest and currently the most intractable issue the Church is facing.

Whenever we open our Bibles we bring our own worlds with us – for good or ill. We always read at a particular time, in a particular place in history and in the context of our personal stories and circumstances. How we listen and respond to what we read will be influenced by all these factors. We will come predisposed to read, hear and respond in certain ways and we may not be conscious when this is happening. That means that the process of faithful, receptive Bible reading requires a developing and honest self-understanding. I want to suggest this is of particular relevance when we discuss human sexuality. We are reading our Bibles and debating faith in the midst of great anxiety.

If I were to trace the personal influences and stories I bring to this present debate (so far as I am aware) I would start with my upbringing as a white, heterosexual male in a British, (largely) middle-class society. From the 1950s onwards, social attitudes began to change with increasing rapidity so I need to beware of generalizing. I attended a single-sex school whose educational ethos centred on particular assumptions about what it meant to 'be a man'. In that private school culture male identity was formed around loyalty to the team, hierarchical authority, competition and toughness as 'character-forming' and suspicion of feelings. More vulnerable emotions were suspect and kept out of sight. Weakness was despised and there was an underlying hostility towards women. Indeed there was a deep anxiety about being thought 'feminine' in any way. Changing-room humour was often sexualized and homophobic. In that world men would generally touch one another affectionately in public only if they had first hit and insulted one another (or after drinking too heavily to care). Nothing must imply any actual attraction of *that* sort. I note in passing that this was the formative educational environment for a large percentage of the political, business and church leaders in recent history. Images of homosexuality at that time ranged between camp caricatures and drag acts to luridly speculative stories of encounters in public toilets. None were in any way positive or respectful. By contrast, I envied what seemed to be the unselfconscious freedom of women to express warmth and affection through touch without fear.

Then came an awakening of faith for which I remain deeply grateful. It led to a call to Christian ministry. I began training at a Bible college where theological studies were built on the pastoral foundation of socially conservative ethics. In that world, homosexuality received very particular condemnation. It was the sin of sins: an 'abomination'. Sodom gave its name to it. Romans chapter 1 expounded it. 'Homosexual' summed up all that was considered most evil, rampantly disordered and wilfully godless in this world. No further discussion was needed, expected or welcomed. Indeed there was an unspoken pressure *not* to talk about it lest the impression was given that this teaching was being questioned in some way. A respected Evangelical leader at the time would speak of homosexuality as 'one of the great evils facing the church' (unaware of how his audience included *good* people secretly anguishing over their own, *un*chosen, sexual attraction). No other subject attracted such opprobrium.

These influences could hardly predispose any young, impressionable Christian men or women to feel comfortable about same-sex relationships. Not only was this condemnation delivered as authoritative, biblical orthodoxy, but it also came with a strong emotional charge and therefore triggered anxiety. It still does. At one level this is to be expected. No one comes neutrally to this subject. Our deepest human identity and securities are tied up in this. This means that, alongside the work of faithful reading and interpreting of Scripture, this debate calls me to listen to my personal journey into a mature and secure awareness of – among other things – my own sexual identity, my relationships and desires. My freedom to read and receive the truth of Scripture will depend, in varying measure, on my willingness to make that journey at all.

A generational feature to this debate has been widely noted. Research shows that many younger Christians simply don't understand the problem at this point. Of course they still have the task of thinking through their discipleship and theology in the midst of an unhelpfully sexualised society. I confess to envying their less defended perspective. As a result they may be more receptive to understandings and responses that previous generations struggle to be trustingly open to.

I can relate to the story of an older Christian telling of how he had come to support faithful same-sex relationships. His church was conservative on this issue but he said his hardest struggle was not with the Bible. He had come to his own convictions about what was and was not taught there on this subject. His struggle was with his own emotional, gut response to the subject – a powerful legacy of his upbringing through a particular era of social, cultural and religious history. He refused to let this response control his interpretation of Scripture, and he was right in this. Revulsion, distress and anxiety are not measures of the rightness of any viewpoint. They are simply telling me I am particularly distressed and anxious about an issue.

Anxiety has been defined by the Merriam-Webster dictionary as

a painful or apprehensive uneasiness of the mind, usually over an impending or anticipated ill; a fearful concern or interest; an abnormal or overwhelming sense of apprehension and fear often marked by physiological signs (as sweating, tension, and increased pulse), by doubt concerning the reality and nature of the threat, and by self-doubt about one's capacity to cope with it.[3]

Anxiety is *my own response* to an issue: *it is not the issue itself.* This is a very important distinction. When anxiety is a driver in my emotional system it will attach to *anything* that unsettles me. Gregory Jantz observed: 'Fear and anxiety are produced by what you tell yourself, not by what you actually experience. For this reason, it is very important to pay attention to what you tell yourself.'[4] This means asking: What is it I fear? What do I think might happen? Is it true? The fear and anxiety have a 'what if' feel. My fear is not so much what has already happened but what I fear *might* happen. Notice the word 'anticipated' in the definition above.

I am reminded of a time when I sought counselling through a time of personal difficulty. During the first few sessions my counsellor mostly listened but at quite regular intervals she stopped me to say, 'Just because you are feeling this it does not mean it is true.' It took me some time to understand what she meant. I had not realized how much I was using my inner anxieties to interpret events in my life. It was a relief to discover there were far less stressful ways of working out the challenges that I was facing at the time.

Other guides through anxiety emphasize the importance of distinguishing between content and process. The content is the information needed for the discussion. The process describes the often hidden emotional responses that drive how we engage with the discussion. The content cannot be faithfully explored unless the underlying processes are recognized. Content has been likened to the tip of the iceberg. The process is the complex of emotions and anxieties beneath the water.

Anxiety shapes our response to issues in a variety of ways. When we are anxious we are 'uptight'. We do not breathe easily. We are not relaxed. Anxiety comes from the same Latin root (*angere*) as the word 'to choke'.

When we are anxious we listen poorly. We are preoccupied with our own concerns. We will be liable to distort what others say without realizing it. In heated exchanges on social media discussions contributors often protest, 'That is not what I said.' I am also hearing-impaired, and I notice that when I am anxious or preoccupied I actually become more deaf. I am less present to people and what they are actually saying.

When we are anxious our mind-set, our responses, will be instinctively regressive and conservative. We will tend to look *back* to find the security we need – where we last remember knowing it. We will assume that the problem is because certain ways of thinking or acting have been abandoned. We will tend to blame others for this.

When we are anxious we need somewhere secure and 'safe' to belong. A strong group instinct can take over. Campaigning groups and organizations proliferate in anxious times. In insecure times there is an attraction to groups within which issues of right and wrong, good or bad, are unambiguously clear and where all speak the same language. Where this happens 'belonging' easily takes priority over engaging with those on the 'outside', with other views.

When we are anxious we need to be in control. We cannot afford to concede any ground to those we disagree with or leave open any possibility that their views may have some substance. We will come across as interfering in the lives and relationships of others. We will need to have the last word.

When we are anxious we struggle to be flexible and to respond imaginatively or creatively in the face of new challenges. (One writer speaks of a 'seatbelt society', oriented toward safety rather than adventure.)

When we are anxious we do not cope well with unresolved questions and uncertainties. We will tend to label others (revisionist, liberal, fundamentalist, homophobic, and so on) rather than actually engage with them. Once they have been labelled, their views are presumed to have been understood and to require no further examination. We will tend to oversimplify the issues.

When we are anxious we will be inhibited from pursuing the trusting, exploratory reflection that Scripture needs for *any* subject. Anxiety is an even poorer guide to recognizing what is true.

When we are anxious it is difficult to manage disagreements and controversies well. It tends to make things worse. I may be unaware that the vigour with which I engage and press my convictions (which may be very well thought out) is not actually centred on the issue itself but on a need to alleviate my anxieties. If I can silence the voices or win the argument my anxieties will be calmed. And they will – for a while.

When we are anxious we will struggle not to hear comments like these as an attack. I stress that is not my intention. I have written of nothing here I have not struggled with myself. Nor am I suggesting that I, or those I disagree with, are simply anxious, but I am noting the high levels of emotion and anxiety that are present in the Church whenever it is trying to discuss sexuality. Time and again debates on social media platforms or blog sites (from all sides of this discussion) start with a genuinely helpful and informed exchange of views, but all too often there seems to come a point when the effort becomes too great, anxiety breaks the surface and the tone becomes increasingly accusatory and dismissive.

One of the more significant gifts to an anxious society and Church has been the continued impact of forms of 'mindfulness' meditation. It is a reminder that the ancient contemplative practices of attentiveness and stillness are needed more than ever today. Our very health and wholeness are under threat. Chronically anxious communities cannot flourish and grow. The task can begin only with a deeper self-understanding. A core aim of mindfulness practice is to enable us be 'more fully aware of our own experience in the present moment in a non-judgemental way'.[5] We need ways of being present to one another and to the challenges of life and faith in non-anxious ways.

Something of that non-judgmental spirit shaped a Church of England project called 'Good Disagreement'. The initiative came from a working group set up to reflect on human sexuality, which published the Pilling Report.[6] It recommended an extended process whereby people from all parts of the Church would meet in small groups for facilitated conversations,

> so that Christians who disagree deeply about the meaning of scripture on questions of sexuality, and on the demands of living in holiness for gay and lesbian people, should understand each other's concerns more clearly and seek to hear each other as authentic Christian disciples.[7]

The journey continues. There are no short cuts.

Not long ago I attended the consecration of a new bishop. It came during a time when a number of bruising debates on conflicted issues were in full flood in the Church. Opinions were divided, and feelings running high. It was easy to feel anxious. Bishops, burdened with the usual messianic expectations (another symptom of anxiety projection), are in the front line of all this. But the service expressed something quite different. It was peaceful, beautiful and holy, and what many remarked on was the quite overwhelming presence of joy. Later that evening the thought came unbidden to me: that a God who gives such joy to his church cannot be anxious. Jesus says to those who follow him, 'Do not worry.'

5

Reading the Bible with Jesus: Midrash, jazz and the continued conversation

There is nothing new going on when we disagree among ourselves about what the Bible says and teaches. Jesus himself often clashed with the religious leaders and teachers of his day. This was partly because of the sheer impact of his presence on the ancient texts. He taught with an immediate, fresh authority, unlike the official teachers, who passed on opinions or theories of interpretation second-hand (Matthew 7.29), but he also interpreted *beyond* the Scriptures: 'You have heard . . . But *I* say to you' (Matthew 5.21–22; my emphasis).

For this Jesus was regarded with intense suspicion by the religious authorities. We read of them trying to trap him. On one occasion a religious lawyer asks him, 'Teacher . . . what must I do to inherit eternal life?' The narrator tells us the question is designed to trip Jesus up, to lay bare whether he is really 'orthodox' (Luke 10.25–37). Jesus does not give him an answer. In typical rabbinic style he asks questions in return: 'What is written in the law? What do you read there?' (v. 26). What does the Bible text say? What is your interpretation of what the text says?

The man replies with the familiar Hebrew summary of faith: 'You shall love the LORD your God with all your heart, and with all your soul, and with all your strength, and with all

35

your mind; and your neighbour as yourself' (Luke 10.27). Jesus says, in effect, 'That is right. Go and do just that.' But the man, 'wanting to justify himself' (v. 29), comes back with another question. This may be a shamelessly self-securing approach to religion, or is it possible that in the presence of Jesus, in spite of himself, a living and questioning faith is surfacing in this man?

The phrase 'love your neighbour' comes from a passage in the book of Leviticus, where 'neighbour' is defined as 'any of your people' (19.18). 'Your neighbour' is therefore anyone within the same particular racial, religious, cultural or kinship group as you. A few verses later the obligation is extended to include 'the alien who resides with you' (Leviticus 19.34). The boundaries of love are clearly prescribed and precisely defined.

Again Jesus gives no answer. Instead – as he so often does at those moments when a direct answer or pronouncement is being sought on what is right or wrong, good or bad – he tells a story (Luke 10.30–37). The story is one of his best known: 'A man was going down from Jerusalem to Jericho . . .' It was a journey through Jewish territory, along a desolate and dangerous desert road. He was robbed, left naked and near death by the side of the road. These are significant details. There is no means of identifying him by race, religion, social status or accent. There is no way of even identifying if he is alive or dead – an important issue in a religion with such strict rules about contamination and purity. He could be *anyone* – and that is the point. He is simply a human being in need.

Two Jewish religious officials take no risks and pass by without stopping. A third traveller appears: a Samaritan. He is therefore already at risk, as he is travelling through a land where his people are hated and subjected to violence. It is not a place to delay, but he stops, bandages the victim and takes him to the nearest inn, which would have been in the Jewish town of Jericho. He pays generously for his care.

Jesus now returns to the question: 'Which of these three, do you think, was a neighbour to the man who fell into the hands of the robbers?' No other answer is possible: 'The one who showed him mercy.' Jesus says to him, 'Go and do likewise' (Luke 10.36–37).

And who actually showed mercy? There would have been real shock as to where this discussion has ended up. For in this story Jesus presents a despised outsider as a role model to devout Jews for the life that God requires – the fulfilling of the law. By contrast, faithful, scrupulously observant religion is exposed as self-justifying, merciless and excluding. By this means Jesus simply dismantles the religious boundaries of neighbourly love taught within his own Scriptures. 'The ethical demands of this vision are limitless.'[1]

And what if Jesus were to ask *us*: 'You know this story. What is *your* reading of it?' Well, Christians have added a word to the description of this story, and the Samaritan neighbour has become the 'good' Samaritan. Why have we done this? That is not how the story describes him. By adding this description we have made the man an exception. The Samaritan is still an outsider, but he is *good*. He has shown mercy. Surely he is not typical? We know that Samaritans are usually all bastards. That one word leaves us free to be impressed, even inspired, without having to change our world-view at all. In this way we reinforce the boundaries of our own prejudice and exclusion to a story that is precisely intended to dismantle them all.

Now, as then, this story blows holes through familiar, securing assumptions about where goodness, faithfulness and the righteous behaviour are to be found in the world. It is not the only time when Jesus' examples of kingdom faith and behaviour reverse the established positions on inclusion and exclusion in radical and controversial ways. It happens repeatedly. The constant scandal is where holiness and goodness and the life of God are to be found. It all keeps falling into the wrong hands.

And it still does.

A very significant proportion of Jesus' teaching is through story-telling: 'he did not speak to them except in parables' (Mark 4.34). In Greek culture, 'parables' were generally allegorical stories with a particular, direct moral point (though the word *parabola* is derived from it, which signifies something that travels by a curved, and thus indirect, route to its target). 'Parable' is likely to be an attempted translation of the Hebrew *mashal*. In Jewish teaching *mashal* is figurative language that uses riddles and allegories. It could be translated 'mysterious speech'. It is oblique, indirect, head-scratching stuff, and was often intentionally confusing or deliberately obscure.

Jesus explains the purpose of parables in precisely this way: that his hearers 'may indeed look, but not perceive, and may indeed listen, but not understand' (Mark 4.12). A better translation of *mashal* would be the Greek word *enigma*. There is one place where the word *enigma* is found in the New Testament – when St Paul writes 'now we see in a mirror, dimly' (1 Corinthians 13.12); the Greek word for 'dimly' is *ainigma*. 'This is an enigma to us' would certainly express the impact of *mashal* story-telling on Jesus' hearers.

We are into a different way of learning and hearing, and of discerning Bible truth. For the first task of *mashal* is to break up our prevailing mindset. We must let go of the preconceived understandings and assumptions we bring with us. It all has to go.

Mashal is an expression of the Jewish approach to Scripture called Midrash. Midrash engages with the Bible as narrative. 'Much of what we call the Bible – the Old and New Testaments – is not a rule book; it is narrative,' says Tom Wright. This changes our understanding of how the Bible teaches:

> Throw a rule book at people's head, or offer them a list of doctrines, and they can duck or avoid it, or simply disagree and go away. Tell them a story though, and you invite them to come into a different world; you invite them to share a world-view or better still a God-view.[2]

That is what Jesus does.

There has been a recovery of the understanding of the Bible as narrative in recent years, but when it comes to discussing difficult or divisive issues we tend to seek pronouncements and instructions: 'The Bible says . . .' But Bible narrative tends to *show* rather than *tell*. It presents rather than expounds or declares. Like the parables, the great historic narratives such as 1 and 2 Samuel are offered as a kind of open theatre, as a form of wisdom-making rather than precise historical record. Narrative leaves things open and is content to leave the story as story. It invites a *continuing* communal reading and exploration in which we, and our world, have a part to play and our own stories to bring.

Those supportive of same-sex relationships are often accused of having been seduced by rationalist Enlightenment thinking instead of faithfully obeying 'what the Bible teaches'. This is based on a popular understanding that the Enlightenment was a wholly secularizing movement, hostile to faith and revelation. While that is true of some aspects of it, David Bebbington makes clear that the historical Evangelical tradition saw itself in a very positive relationship with Enlightenment thinking and that this especially influenced its approach to the Bible.[3] Didactic and empirical analytical methods for studying the texts became important. These have their place of course, but one outcome was the tendency to approach the Bible with the assumption that there is one message and one meaning, and that it contains definitive, univocal conclusions that apply to all people at all times.

Tom Wright warns against the assumption that what the Bible teaches on any issue can be determined by simply reading a Bible text or verse as if that were proof:

> First, there is an implied, and quite unwarranted, positivism: we imagine that we are 'reading the text, straight', and that if somebody disagrees with us it must be because they, unlike we ourselves, are secretly using 'presuppositions' of this or that sort. This is simply naive, and actually astonishingly arrogant and dangerous. It fuels the second point. Evangelicals often use the phrase 'authority of scripture' when they *mean* the authority of Evangelical, or Protestant, theology, since the assumption is made that we (Evangelicals, or Protestants) are the ones who know and believe what the Bible is saying . . . the phrase 'authority of scripture' can, by such routes, come to mean simply 'the authority of Evangelical tradition, as opposed to Catholic or rationalist ones'.[4]

It is one reason why biblical debates can so quickly become deadlocked.

Another outcome of Enlightenment influence has been the tendency to prioritize text over story. One example of this is found in the centrality of the expository tradition as the primary way of teaching Scripture. This is based on the belief that 'the revelation of the purpose of God in Scripture should be sought primarily in its didactic rather than its descriptive parts'. This means that 'we should look for it in the teaching of Jesus, and in the sermons and writings of the apostles rather than in the purely narrative portions'.[5]

But this is surely the reverse of how Jesus taught? The greater proportion of his teaching was through story. When the story is used only to illustrate a didactic point it is being asked to serve a prior context and frame of meaning. The story is not allowed to speak on its own terms and so it loses its power to surprise, shock or subvert. Nothing new can break through. In this way stories become a way of illustrating our preconceived views.

By contrast Jonathan Pennington pictures the Gospels as being like the keystone in a Roman archway. The keystone is vital for holding together the two sides of the archway – the Old and New Testaments – and so for holding the whole structure together and enabling it to function as an entryway. In this way, 'the fourfold witness of the Gospels provides the guiding principle and lodestar for understanding and standing under all of Holy Scripture'.[6]

The image of a keystone should not, however, imply a single controlling meaning running through the whole structure. Nor is that the approach of Midrash. Rather than seeking certainties and unchanging truths, Midrash keeps the questions open and is not threatened by disagreements. Above all it offers a creative and imaginative way of connecting ancient

Scriptures with the challenges of life and faith today. All voices are welcome. So in the process of meeting around the text we may grow in empathy and understanding and in our relationships with one another.

Midrash has been likened to jazz: 'This jazz is not just an experiment or whim, but emerges from a thoroughgoing knowledge of the tradition. By this means a creative dialogue is set up which permits something fresh, engaging and new.'[7] In the same way, says David Ford, Midrash 'does not compete with the plain sense of the text but improvises with it in relation to some new context, issue or event' by 'taking the plain sense seriously but going beyond it, linking it to other texts, asking new questions of it, extending the meaning, discovering depths and applications that have not been suggested before'.[8] There is a process of faithful improvisation, even play. In so doing the text is given life and given new applicability in our context. As with jazz this improvising is not 'making it up'. It requires a strong commitment to the original text and tradition, but thereafter, Midrash, like jazz, allows many possibilities. 'Bible' is, after all, a plural word. To read it is to listen to a wide variety of voices in very varied contexts.

There is an ancient form of Bible reading that proceeds as a gentle, prayerful Midrash. It is called Lectio Divina (divine reading). In this method (individually or in a group) a Bible passage is approached in a spirit of receptive trust and openness: it is no ordinary text; it is alive with God.

The passage is slowly read three times. After each reading a question is invited and a time of silence and listening follows. Nothing is forced. After the first reading we are asked to locate ourselves in what we have heard and to consider: 'What word or phrase or image has touched my heart as I have read this passage?' After the second reading we ask: 'In what way am I "hearing" or "seeing" Christ in this passage?' After the third reading we are to reflect: 'In what way is Christ calling me (or us) forth in this passage – to new life, relationships and understanding?' The most formative gift of this way of reading the Bible is that it teaches us to read Scripture in the presence of Jesus, open to what is new and willing to follow.

Head-scratching *mashal* bewilderment well describes the struggles many are having with the Bible as received understandings of sexuality and relationships are being challenged in unsettling ways. Indeed, we must beware of assuming that this unsettling breaking-up process belonged only to the early Christian Church and is now complete; that from this safe distance we now know and can read the 'real' meaning of things. When we do that we remain as closed and resistant as the first religious authorities.

This is a struggle in the presence of Christ. It is he who tells our stories. And we can trust him in this place and with this process as we, in our time, hear the stories of radical, merciful inclusion.

Like Jesus, we must let goodness and love fall into the 'wrong' hands.

6

'Lie the lyings of a woman': seeking the meaning of Leviticus 18.22

The book of Leviticus is the ancient code of law of the Hebrew people providing detailed guidance for the day-to-day life and worship of the people of God. Its overriding priority is purity and holiness – for God is holy. So there is a very particular concern for the avoidance of what was believed to defile and render people impure before God. These related to health and included dietary matters such as not eating shellfish (11.9–12); environmental concerns such as agriculture and harvesting (19.9); and the maintaining of boundaries around human and sexual relationships (20.9–21).

Some laws clearly reflect the limited understandings of an ancient culture, such as concerns about the shedding of blood by women during menstruation (15.19–33). Some laws, such as the exclusion of people with deformities and disabilities (21.16–23), are now rightly considered offensive – certainly not as being God's law for us today. Both the content of the laws and the severity with which they are laid down are strange to modern ears. Positively, these are examples from an ancient and differently ordered world of what it meant to honour the absolute priority of God and the hard work of faithful, consecrated living.

Chapter 18 contains this particular prohibition: 'You shall not lie with a male as with a woman; it is an abomination' (v. 22).

The verse is repeated in chapter 20 verse 13, with the addition of the death penalty for both men involved. The lawgiver offers no reason or further clarification. It is clearly not a matter for discussion. He expects his hearers to understand and obey.

English translations tend to give the impression that the meaning of this verse is clear and uncomplicated. That has contributed to the long-held belief that these verses unambiguously prohibit any and all same-sex relationships (whether or not the death penalty was still thought to be required). In fact this understanding of the text did not become established in the churches in Europe until the Middle Ages. The truth is that the Hebrew is extremely difficult to translate with any clarity. In more recent times both Jewish and Christian commentators have become more cautious about claiming what this teaching actually means.

A literal rendering of the Hebrew in chapter 18, verse 22, reads:

With a male you shall not lie the lyings of a woman. That [or 'it'] [is an] abomination.[1]

It is immediately clear that this verse is difficult to render intelligibly in idiomatic English. So what does it actually mean?

The NRSV translation quoted above is one of the few to correctly translate 'male' and 'woman'. The great majority of Bible versions translate 'man' and 'woman', even though in the Hebrew the more general 'male' (*zakhar*) is used, not 'man' (*ish*). Just as 'man' and 'woman' are usually paired, 'male' is usually contrasted with 'female' (*neqevah*), but here 'male' is contrasted with 'woman' (or wife, *ishah*). This is very uncommon and surely intentional. The meaning and purpose of this law would

46

presumably have been clear to the original hearers or it would have come with more clarification. Modern readers need more help, however.

It is possible that 'male' could refer to a young boy and that pederasty or other coercive sexual activity is meant here. Some have suggested that concerns about incest underlie this choice of words. As the majority of English translations mask the complexities of this verse altogether, modern readers may struggle to see why this needs discussing at all. There appears to be carefully selective wordplay in this text. Read from our considerable historical, cultural and linguistic distance, the passage is very difficult to understand with any precision.

A review of translations and commentaries, both Jewish and Christian, reveals multiple possible understandings as to who or what is condemned here.[2] These include:

- same-sex eroticism ('homosexuality');
- sexual intercourse between males;
- anal penetration between males;
- the active/insertive partner in anal intercourse;
- the passive/receptive partner in anal intercourse;
- male cultic prostitution;
- gender confusion (male acting as a female);
- social humiliation (male treated as a female);
- failure to ensure procreation (waste of semen);
- male–male incest.

The first of these is the most relevant to our context and the most commonly assumed meaning, but it is also the most problematic. For if the writer's intention were to declare a total prohibition on sex between men, he could have said so very simply: 'With a male you shall not lie' (the law is addressed to men). The addition of the words *mishkevey ishshah* ('as with a woman') suggests a more specific focus of concern. For this reason studies of this text increasingly question whether this law has any applicability or relevance to our contemporary understanding of homosexuality.

Nevertheless, this assumption continues to be found, even in scholarly studies. When he comes to this text in his weighty Bible commentary on Leviticus, John E. Hartley simply writes, 'Homosexuality is forbidden (cf. Romans 1:27; 1 Corinthians 6:9).'[3] He offers no grounds for making the statement in this context. In several places in this book I argue that the two New Testament texts he cites in support are not about homosexuality either (see Chapters 7, 8 and 11). Robert Gagnon also uses 'homosexual' and 'homosexuality' throughout his studies of these texts. He further claims that 'the level at which the critical laws stigmatize and criminalize all homosexual intercourse goes far beyond anything else currently known in the ancient Near East'.[4] He is correct in noting the distinctive conservatism of the Hebrew laws on sexual behaviour, but he is wrong, like Hartley, to use the word 'homosexual' to translate these texts. The Bible never calls 'homosexuality' an abomination, for the word refers to a concept of sexual orientation that was not known until several thousand years later. These verses are concerned with certain *actions*, and it is actions that are addressed here.

So, briefly, what are the other possibilities? Leviticus is a working out of faithful, consecrated living in God's good creation. It builds on Genesis. So some have suggested that the prohibition on men having sex with men relates to the creation imperative to have children – to fill the earth (Genesis 1.28). As same-sex intercourse cannot conceive life, it contradicts the intention at the heart of human creation. The prohibition makes no mention of procreation, however. So it could be argued that what is being condemned here is not 'male–male sexual contact in general, but only anal penetration and, probably, only of anal penetration of a free Israelite citizen'.[5]

The exclusive focus on *male* sexual behaviour and male understandings of gender roles suggests another significance. Gagnon claims that 'lying with a man as with a woman' means 'to treat a man as though his masculine identity counted for nothing . . . as though he were not a man but a woman'.[6] He appears to be endorsing an ancient and biblical understanding of sexual roles in terms of assertive/passive, possession/submission (and therefore male/female), but does this in any way reflect a contemporary Christian understanding of human social or sexual relating at all? Put simply, homosexuality is not about men behaving like women, or treating other men like women. It is not *just* about men either. All of this suggests that the original concerns behind this prohibition lie elsewhere.

Another possibility concerns beliefs about purity and social ordering. Purity, in that ancient world, was believed to be a matter of keeping things separate; impurity came from mixing. Certain behaviours were resisted if they symbolically or actually crossed boundaries or confused 'categories' believed to be part of the original creation. Within that world a man lying 'as with a woman' is declared to be a crossing of that boundary.

We can begin to discern what this teaching in Leviticus contributes to modern expressions of relating and intimacy only if we have clarity about what it meant in its original context. A law can be faithfully (and safely) applied to very different societies and times in history only when its original underlying intent has been established. Discussions about which of the Old Testament purity laws should and should not be obeyed began with Jesus and remained a source of tension in the first Christian churches.

In relation to the Hebrew purity laws, Brownson discerns three broad movements within the New Testament, which were often initiated by teachings and example of Jesus himself. They are movements:

- away from defining purity externally and towards defining purity in terms of the motives and dispositions of the heart [see, for example, Jesus' teaching in Matthew 15.17–20];
- away from defensiveness and separateness and towards confidence and engagement;
- away from a backwards look towards the old creation, and a shifting to a forwards look towards the new creation.[7]

In her book *Scripture, Ethics and Same-Sex Relationships*, Karen Keen explores the 'process that we must undertake to rightly interpret and apply biblical laws today'.[8] The key lies in understanding the original intent. What meaning and purpose might emerge if we approached Leviticus 18.22 in the same way? Might we be able to discern something of its original intent and thus how it could be applied to relationships today? In this way, we seek to be faithful to the original intent of a law but quite possibly in ways that the ancient world could not have imagined.[9]

If we place Leviticus 18.22 within the scriptural movements of which Brownson speaks, Keen asks, 'are there alternative ways to fulfil that intent more fully that take into consideration the predicament of gay and lesbian people'?[10] I think we have to be honest. This remains work in progress. There are clear grounds for saying that we do not have enough background yet to understand this verse: 'The social and cultural significance of this verse within its ancient context is still waiting to be uncovered.'[11] My own view is that a reverent agnosticism rightly surrounds the interpretations of this text.

After a long, learned online discussion on this text, a contributor suggested to his fellow debaters:

> At the end of the day, there are simply some linguistic questions that we can't definitively answer given our present, non-native knowledge of the ancient language; and which of our readings is closer to the ancient usage is, I fear, one of them. I think we've reached an impasse on the issue of how best to understand mishkebe ishshah ['as with a woman'] in these two verses [Leviticus18.22 and 23.11].[12]

The response of some was to claim that there are therefore no clear grounds for changing the traditional understanding of the texts. But given this lack of certainty, there are surely no grounds for *imposing* the traditional view, any more than there are for excluding those with disabilities on the basis of clearer texts.

7

Romans and the wrath of God: who was Paul writing about?

'For the wrath of God is revealed from heaven against all ungodliness and wickedness' (Romans 1.18). So begins Paul's famous denunciation of the godless, Gentile culture in his world and its terrible consequences. What follows is a theological and moral critique of a shamelessly indulgent society where all moral order or conviction has collapsed. This includes a passage long believed to contain the most explicit and unambiguous condemnation of homosexuality.

The first questions to ask of any Bible passage are always: what does the passage actually say, who was it first written for, what situation is it seeking to address (and why) and, so far as we can discern, how would it have been understood by the original audience? In that light, we can begin to explore the relevance of the passage for our own discipleship and context. That is the focus of my reflections in this chapter rather than offering yet another extended and detailed exposition of the whole text.

Paul's letter was written to the church in Rome, the majority of whom were Gentile believers. The first church there had consisted entirely of Jewish Christians but they were expelled from Rome by the emperor Claudius (around AD 49). They returned after his death but were now a significant minority in the church community there and even more so in the midst of that great and powerful and pagan city. Jewish–Gentile tensions were apparent here as elsewhere in the New Testament churches. So

Paul wrote a pastoral and theological letter addressing these concerns and teaching the whole Church that Gentiles were indeed part of the fulfilling of the gospel promised by God through Abraham.

Shortly into the letter, Paul's tone changes abruptly. He adopts a particular style of speech called 'rhetoric' and appears to side with a minority racial and cultural group in that church – conservative Jewish believers (Romans 1.18–32). Rhetoric is a familiar way to rally and unite the faithful. It tends to use broad-brush assertions to make its points, and was as familiar in Roman culture as it is in public life today. Indeed reading these verses aloud as if to rouse a partisan crowd is one way of getting the feel of Paul's style. He deliberately creates an 'us' and 'them' effect, 'them' being the wicked world out there and 'us' the faithful Christian minority that has kept itself pure and separate from such appalling, shameful behaviour. It is easy to imagine those Jewish believers, vulnerable and anxious as they were, enjoying this robust take-down of the Gentile world around them, being reaffirmed in their own godliness and glad of a spiritual leader who was not afraid to 'tell it like it is'. And that is precisely what Paul intends. The passage includes these verses:

Therefore God gave them up in the lusts of their hearts to impurity, to the degrading of their bodies among themselves, because they exchanged the truth about God for a lie and worshipped and served the creature rather than the Creator, who is blessed for ever! Amen. For this reason God gave them up to degrading passions. Their women exchanged natural intercourse for unnatural, and in the same way also the men, giving up natural intercourse with women, were consumed with passion for one another.

Men committed shameless acts with men and received in their own persons the due penalty for their error. (Romans 1.24–27)

Rome was a city full of temples dedicated to the worship of a bizarre range of creatures and deities. One particularly notorious cult was devoted to the goddess Cybele. Cybelenes practised cross-dressing and indulged in sexual excess of every kind. Their behaviour was so scandalous that the Roman Senate sought to ban the cult. At the frenzied height of their gatherings male devotees were known to castrate themselves. It is very possible that Paul was referring to this when he refers to their having 'received in their own persons the due penalty for their error' (Romans 1.27). All this would have been common knowledge in the local church and would be brought to mind as Paul's letter was read. Surely this was where Gentile living ended up, with God's judgement revealed.

Who was Paul referring to in his very specific denunciation of that sexual behaviour? These are people who:

- have wilfully and knowingly turned from their Creator to forms of idolatrous living;
- have, in consequence, been given over by God as judgement (Romans 1.24), which seems to result in the removal of any restraining grace or moral sensibility on human desire and behaviour;
- are therefore acting out of uncontrolled, burning, inflamed and unbridled lust; and
- are acting contrary to 'nature' – specifically, they have deliberately exchanged 'natural' (other-sex) sexual behaviour for an 'unnatural' (same-sex) one.

So much is perfectly clear from the text. We now need to ask in what way Paul's words can be applied in our modern context, in particular, what relevance this teaching has for a same-sex couple:

- who have turned *towards*, not away from, God, as committed followers of Christ;
- whose lives reveal the blessing of God and the fruit of the Spirit, and who are plainly not wallowing in a godless moral vacuum;
- whose loving commitment to one another reflects the same faithfulness and consecration to which their married heterosexual friends aspire;
- for whom the love of a companion of the same sex is entirely innate and 'natural', that is, there has been no 'exchange'.

Since Paul describes behaviour involving choice and exchange, he is arguably not referring at all to people whom we would now consider to be homosexual. It seems more likely that he is describing heterosexual people indulging in anal sex (and much else besides in that context of rampant and unrestrained promiscuity).

The passage also provides an example of how the 'plain meaning' of the text may be misleading. When Paul writes, 'Their women exchanged natural intercourse for unnatural' (Romans 1.26), readers today will assume that he is referring to lesbian sex. For the first four centuries of the Church, however, all Bible commentators, including Augustine of Hippo and Clement of Alexandria, assumed that Paul was referring to women who were having anal sex with their husbands (or with other men). None of these commentators interpreted this as a reference to lesbianism. Modern understandings of Bible texts are not always the same as the original ones.

Then there is Paul's argument from 'nature'. For Paul, people exchanging their natural (other-sex) desires for unnatural (same-sex) ones is against nature (Romans 1.26–27). He sees no need to explain further, but seems to be basing his case here on the Genesis creation stories. 'Nature' and 'natural' thus mean 'as originally created'. It is not clear what Paul is drawing on by way of evidence. Elsewhere in this book I note that our understanding of science, biology and much else must inform our reading of Scripture. There are huge and complex areas of insight into human development and identity in the natural world that Paul would have had no knowledge of in his time.

In another letter, Paul appeals to nature to teach about personal appearances. After claiming that it will be obvious to all that women should have their heads covered ('Judge for yourselves'!), he continues, 'Does not nature itself teach you that if a man wears long hair, it is degrading to him' (1 Corinthians 11.13, 14). The answer today, across long periods of history and in many parts of the world, would be 'no'. 'Nature' in this verse must mean 'prevailing social custom' or what might otherwise be called 'normal' behaviour. Within more traditional cultures, to ignore social or religious norms can cause serious scandal and Paul was always concerned to avoid placing any obstacle in the way of the gospel. A parallel may be found in a Western man or woman living abroad in a highly traditional non-Christian culture. Their clothing and lifestyle will be chosen to conform and to avoid departing from what is considered 'natural' in that society. The length of a man's hair is surely related to local custom rather than being a decree for every place and time – though I recall a discussion with someone who was deeply concerned that the fashion for men to have longer hair made them look like women. Scripture taught that it was degrading, he said, and it caused sexual confusion. On the wall behind him as he spoke were portraits of some of the historic heroes of the faith, all of whom had longer hair than anyone present in the room. No one ever accused John Wesley or John the Baptist of spreading sexual confusion by their hairstyles.[1]

So the appeal to what is 'natural' needs to be made with great care. It is perilously easy to believe that what is most familiar, right and preferable to us is surely the most 'natural' ordering of things, whereas it may simply reveal the narrow boundaries of our world and life experience. We may need to get out more! I remember the reaction of someone the first time they saw a woman wearing a clerical collar. 'It's not natural,' they muttered, with some anger. What they actually meant was 'I have never seen this before. It is not part of my world and I am very uncomfortable with it'.

There are similar problems with the word 'normal'. 'Normal' generally describes the behaviour of the majority. Its opposite is wholly pejorative – 'abnormal'. The word stigmatizes and excludes. But there is nothing wrong per se with someone who is behaving in ways outside the norm. They are simply being different. So I find it more helpful to speak of what is 'typical'. What is not typical is simply atypical. There is nothing necessarily wrong with that. When Marcus Green wrote of his experience of being gay in the Church he called his book *The Possibility of Difference* (2018).

Precisely.

We do not know how the Gentile Christians felt listening to Paul's words about their own culture. In the same way, those who are heterosexual have no way of knowing what it is like for gay Christians to hear this passage read, preached and debated in a way that leaves them feeling forever tainted by association with the most extreme, antisocial, godless sexual behaviour. 'I was brought up Evangelical Protestant', writes theologian James Alison, 'and this text, Romans 1, was really a text of terror for me, a text in some way associated with a deep emotional and spiritual annihilation, something inflicting paralysis.'[2] A Christian man in his seventies writes:

> The prohibitions in Leviticus and St Paul (let alone Sodom) do not even come near to what I know and experience in my relationship with my partner of thirty-six totally happy years. I believe these biblical texts are condemning something else that I have known and experienced once upon a time, but not now . . . I am quite certain that the writers do not know anything of same-sex life together of 'mutual society, help and comfort'.

In fact, the earliest known exposition of the Romans passage, from the second century, assumes that Paul is talking about pederasty – men abusing boys or slaves – a routine practice in Roman society:

> For those who have set up a market for fornication and established infamous resorts for the young for every kind of vile pleasure, who do not abstain even from males, males with males committing shocking abominations . . . These adulterers and pederasts defame the eunuchs and the once-married.[3]

So we need to be very careful in discerning how this passage can be applied to Christians today who find themselves homosexual by 'nature', confess Christ as Lord, repent of their sins and renounce evil; who are faithful and chaste in their relationships; and who seek blessing on their same-sex partnership and their shared discipleship in the way of Christ.

Meanwhile, in rhetorical full flow, Paul offers an extended list of vices that function as a kind of summing up of his case against the whole revolting Gentile culture. The list includes evils like envy, deceit, craftiness, gossip, being rebellious towards one's parents, foolishness, heartlessness and ruthlessness. Sex makes no appearance at all! At this point you might wonder if his Jewish hearers have started to notice how Paul's judgement list was suddenly edging uncomfortably closer to home.

He has now reached the pivotal moment in his argument, but for modern readers it is immediately derailed by the clumsy chapter and verse divisions in the text. At the very point Paul makes his startling, rhetorical shift in focus chapter 1 finishes and chapter 2 starts in a text that was originally continuous. There were no chapter or verse divisions in the original text. Paul is in mid-argument:

> *They* [the Gentiles] know God's decree . . . yet *they* not only do them but even applaud others who practise them. Therefore *you* have no excuse, whoever *you* are, when *you* judge others; for in passing judgement on another *you* condemn yourself, because *you*, the judge, are doing the very same things. (1.32–2.1; my emphasis)

The switch is shocking – and it is meant to be. From denouncing 'they', Paul suddenly turns and without warning addresses 'you'. So, after hearing Gentiles roundly condemned, Jewish believers find themselves under the same judgement! This is the moment Paul has been leading up to. He turns on the Jews for their critical, judgemental attitude towards Gentile believers: 'You have no excuse!' (Romans 2.1). The shift is given even more force by the switch from the plural 'them' to the singular 'you'. Some commentators think that he might even be speaking to a particular leader of the Jewish believers' group. The letter continues to challenge any notions of spiritual superiority: 'Are we any better off? No, not at all . . . since all have sinned and fall short of the glory of God' (Romans 3.9, 23).

So how might Paul write this letter to today's Church?[4] He would be just as trenchant in his critique of idolatry, promiscuity, power and injustice wherever he finds it. But rhetoric works only if your audience already agrees with your view of things. What Paul is describing must be self-evidently wrong and in no need of further explanation to his followers. Paul portrays this sexual activity as a deliberate rejection of God. For Paul, 'Godless living and shameful sexual behaviour go together. Immoral sexual behaviour is a sign and symptom of the Godless life.'[5] This line of argument simply does not transfer to our own church, however. The link Paul makes between the recognition of God, sexual desire and behaviour does not hold for gay Christians today any more than it does for heterosexual believers.

Today, Paul would have the opportunity to meet couples in committed, faithful, and stable homosexual relationships that are growing all the fruits of love, joy, peace, kindness and self-control about which he wrote. He would probably still not come easily to this, but might he not be willing to reflect in new ways on how homosexual Christian people are best enabled to order and consecrate their desires? For, as he himself taught, 'it is better to marry than to be aflame with passion' (1 Corinthians 7.9) and 'it is not good [to] be alone'

(Genesis 2.18). Paul might extend his developing vision for human relationships based on love, mutuality and partnership to gay Christians and away from the male-centred, patriarchal ordering of the Hebrew Scriptures on the one hand and the dominance/submissive practices of surrounding pagan culture on the other.

Finally, Paul would be as fierce as ever in rebuking the Church when it assumes any kind of superiority and stands in judgement over the lives of others. There is still no excuse (Romans 2.1).

This epistle rightly sits at the theological heart of the New Testament. The vision and priorities expounded within it are as central as ever to Christian life and mission, but is this letter concerned at all with homosexuality – at least in the way we understand the word today? A redeemed rereading of this epistle is required if it is to speak faithfully and pastorally to the context of today's Church and world.

8

On giving it a name:
the origin of the word 'homosexual'

In 1869, a small publisher in Leipzig published a pamphlet arguing against Paragraph 143 of the Prussian legal code, which legislated against same-sex relationships. Until this point in its history, Germany had been a loose confederation of states, each with its own legal system, some based on the more liberal Napoleonic Code and others, like that of Prussia, being more conservative. As Germany moved towards becoming a unified nation, one of the debates was about same-sex relationships and there was concern that Prussia might influence other states in a more conservative direction. The author's fears proved well founded when, in 1871, the new German Criminal Code came into being. Prussia's Paragraph 143 became the national Paragraph 175. In this newly unified nation, sexual relationships between men were now a criminal offence.

The author of the pamphlet was a journalist called Karl-Maria Kertbeny. Kertbeny was concerned to find a new name for those drawn to same-sex relationships. He wanted a more neutral term to replace the ones in common use, some of which were simply descriptive but others of which were discriminatory or contemptuous (for example 'criminal against nature', 'bugger', 'sodomite' and 'degenerate').

Kertbeny coined a number of words. Two of them survived to become standard words in the vocabulary for sexuality and gender discussions – 'homosexual' and 'heterosexual'. He seems to have been a troubled man in his own relationships, and we do not know exactly what he meant by these words. Kertbeny is credited with the first appearance in history of the word 'homosexual' as a term to categorize people who are erotically attracted to those of the same sex.

Fast-forward to the USA in the 1930s. A committee of translators were working on a new English Bible translation to create a version that was more readable and accessible. They had reached 1 Corinthians 6.9–10, where Paul lists ten behaviours that come under the judgement of God and exclude people from the kingdom of God. Included in this list are two Greek words *arsenokoitai* and *malakoi* (I discuss these words further in Chapter 10). They were commonly taken to refer to active and passive roles in same-sex sexual activity. One of the senior translators working on the new translation, William Moffatt, had translated the words as 'catamite' and 'sodomite' in his 1922 translation of the Bible.

The committee did two things. They assumed (as many had before them) that the two words were actually paired in that passage – though no other words in the list are. They then went looking for one word to unite the two. The archives of the committee chair reveal a man who kept highly detailed notes of *everything* (including his meals), but there is no record of their discussion at this point. We do not know if they considered any other words. We only know that they finally chose the word 'homosexual'.

When the new Revised Standard Version (RSV) was published in 1946 it was the first Bible translation in *any* language to use the word 'homosexual' to translate certain words or phrases from the Hebrew and Greek Bible texts. We do not know what the committee understood by the word 'homosexual', or why they thought this recently coined word was suitable for translating words and phrases describing certain sexual behaviour in ancient texts. The RSV was widely reviewed on publication but this novel translation seems to have gone unnoticed or was simply accepted without discussion.[1] The USA in the 1930s was only just beginning to explore the idea of sexuality and sexual identity, and homosexuality was being treated as a mental illness or judged to be a moral degeneracy. In many states same-sex sexual intercourse was a criminal offence under sodomy laws. Kinsey's groundbreaking research on *Sexual Behavior in the Human Male*, the first attempt to look scientifically at the subject of sexuality, was not published until 1948.

Meanwhile, back in Germany, at the very moment the RSV translators were making their fateful choice of translation, Kertbeny's worst fears were being realized. Paragraph 175 was being used by the Nazis to round up gay men, unknown thousands of whom were persecuted, imprisoned, castrated or killed in concentration camps. The main reason for their persecution was that they were deemed to corrupt German values and culture by not contributing to the fertility and growth of the pure Aryan race.

The RSV, with its innovative use of the word 'homosexual', quickly became a highly influential English Bible translation. Translations that followed the RSV added other words as well: 'perverts' (RSV, 1962), 'those who practise homosexuality' (NIV, 1978) and 'men who have sex with men' (CEV, 1995).

The same trend is evident in the use of other terms. For example, earlier translations of *malakoi* included 'weak', 'wanton', 'unchaste' and 'effeminate'. Modern translations now included 'passive homosexual partners', 'male prostitutes' and 'sexual pervert'. This is very significant. *Arsenokoitai* and *malakoi*, if rightly paired, originally described *roles* being played in a same-sex sexual act. A very specific judgement was being made in the passage. Understanding the original context and its purpose is crucial to understanding what the passage says. What the original Greek words do not appear to be doing is describing what we would call the sexual *orientation* of a person, which is itself a very modern concept.

Having once appeared in 1 Corinthians 6.9, in a wholly negative context of severe judgement, the word 'homosexual' became attached to Bible texts that variously describe abusive, exploitative or idolatrous expressions of sexual behaviour. There are many more examples of abusive sexual behaviour by heterosexual men in the Bible, but to be a heterosexual male in itself is never assumed to be the problem. The same is not applied to the word 'homosexual'. A word coined to describe a particular expression of human relating has been used to translate ancient texts that originally judged a particular sexual activity. The Bible texts always focus on the action, not the person, but this distinction becomes lost in translation. The condemnation of particular sexual *roles* now becomes a general condemnation of a certain kind of *person*.

All of this warns us that much more care is needed before it can be claimed that 'the Church has taught the same thing about homosexuality for 2,000 years' or that the Bible 'everywhere teaches against homosexuality'. The word 'homosexual' did not exist anywhere before 1869 and does not appear in any Bible translation until 1946. The word itself does not appear in the Bible at all. The texts that are assumed to teach that homosexual relationships are wrong, in every case, describe forms of sexual subjugation through rape or violence, excessive lustful behaviour, patterns of coercive male dominance or a disregarding of acceptable norms of social and religious behaviour.

9

The sin of Sodom: when names become labels

Situated on the fertile plains of the Jordan Valley, Sodom was surely once a city of wealth and beauty, but it enters the ancient Bible texts as a place of malign reputation, under the imminent judgement of God (Genesis 13.10–13).

The drama of Sodom's destruction is told in Genesis 19, but the key to understanding these notorious events are found in the previous chapter, where the story properly begins. There 'the Lord appeared to Abraham [with two strangers] by the oaks of Mamre, as he sat at the entrance of his tent in the heat of the day' (Genesis 18.1). Note that Abraham offers the strangers every hospitality, for what happens in Sodom will stand in precise contrast to what is happening here in Abraham's tent. There is much else to say about the fuller context of this story, but the issue that concerns us here is Sodom's iconic identification with the supposed presence of homosexuality and God's presumed judgement on it: 'The destruction of Sodom in Genesis 19 has been used to justify the systematic persecution of people in homoerotic relationships. No other biblical text has had such sinister repercussions for so-called sexual minorities.'[1]

After resting with Abraham, the two men (now revealed as angels) travel on to Sodom, where they meet Lot 'sitting in the gateway of Sodom' (Genesis 19.1). He offers them generous hospitality and refuge. It is now night and the town is not a safe place for strangers. The parallels between Abraham and Lot sitting at entrances and offering hospitality to strangers are clearly deliberate.

News quickly spreads of Lot's guests and the men of the city (Genesis 19.4) converge on Lot's house and demand access to them. They make their intentions frighteningly clear: they want to rape them. Lot refuses, insisting that he must honour the hospitality he has offered. He must have been in a very vulnerable position as an outsider himself, but his offer of his underage daughters to the men instead of his guests is one of the most horrific and neglected aspects of this story. How are we to understand a society in which the obligation to honour male guests is so paramount that a father will offer his own daughters to rapists rather than breach this code? Just as the mob are on the point of breaking down the door the angels strike them blind and insist that Lot and his family flee immediately. The town is beyond saving.

The assumption has long been that the sin of the town was unrestrained homosexual lust and desire. That the town is destroyed by God for its behaviour has simply served to confirm the extreme seriousness with which homosexuality is judged by God. In fact the context is clearly more one of gang violence and subjugation than of sexual desire. Used in this way, rape is an expression of power, not of sexual desire. It is a means of humiliating and disgracing the victims and remains a common feature of war and ethnic violence in modern times.

The Hebrew Bible speaks often of the fate of Sodom. It is regularly held up as a warning to present and later generations. In addressing the crisis of his exiled people, Ezekiel makes repeated comparisons with the sin of Sodom:

This was the guilt of your sister Sodom: she and her daughters had pride, excess of food, and prosperous ease, but did not aid the poor and needy. They were haughty, and did abominable things before me; therefore I removed them when I saw it. (Ezekiel 16.49–50)

Isaiah calls Israel's leaders 'you rulers of Sodom' and condemns them specifically for not defending the orphans and widows: 'your hands are full of blood . . . seek justice' (Isaiah 1.10, 15, 17). The focus of judgement is clear. Sodom's sin is inhospitality, injustice and idolatry. Although words like 'adultery' are often used *metaphorically* to speak of Israel's faithless behaviour towards God, the Hebrew Scriptures nowhere speak of the sin of Sodom as sexual in any way, let alone *homo*sexual.

That hospitality, not homosexuality, is the issue at Sodom is made clear by Lot's response to the people's demands. He does not say, 'Do not do this because homosexuality is wrong' or even 'Do not do this because rape is wrong', but 'Do nothing to these men, for they have come under the shelter of my roof' (Genesis 19.8). Furthermore, the text repeatedly stresses that the entire male population of the town was present outside Lot's door: 'The men of the city, the men of Sodom, both young and old, all the people to the last man, surrounded the house' (19.4). To read this as a story about homosexual sin requires us to assume that the entire male population of Sodom was gay.

Sodom is mentioned nine times in the New Testament. Once again the judgement consistently concerns the failure of hospitality towards the messengers from God. Jesus actually rates the evils of Sodom as less serious than what the town of Capernaum has done in not believing the signs they are seeing (Matthew 11.23–24).

There are only two places in the entire Bible that link the sin of Sodom to sex in a non-metaphorical sense. The letter of Jude contains a brief passage about disobedient angels 'who did not keep their own position' and are now held 'in deepest darkness' (vv. 6, 7). He links this to the people of Sodom who, 'in a similar manner to these, having given themselves over to sexual immorality and gone after strange flesh' (v. 7, NKJV). The issue appears to be sex with angels. There is a possible allusion to Genesis 6.2–4 where, in the context of divine concern about the growing wickedness on the earth, 'the sons of God went in to the daughters of humans' (v. 4). The second letter of Peter appears to follow Jude with a reference to 'those who indulge their flesh in depraved lust' (2 Peter 2.10). Linguistically and theologically, both writers appear to be following writings from the period between the Old and New Testament at this point rather than the original Hebrew Scriptures. This may be the way of understanding their concerns more clearly.

But English translations easily mislead here. Out of thirty translations, only ten follow the literal (and specific) translation – 'strange flesh' – in Jude. Others speak variously of 'acted immorally and indulged in unnatural lust' (CEV), 'gave themselves up to sexual immorality and perversion' (NIV), 'indulged in sexual immorality and perversion' (GNB), 'committed all sorts of sexual sins' (CEV) and 'filled with immorality and every kind of sexual perversion' (NLT). These translations are so speculative and far from the original as to border on irresponsibility at times. We should also note that these texts could be equally or more concerned with heterosexual than with homosexual behaviour. It has also been observed that 'strange flesh' is not at all a likely synonym for homosexual sex, where the concern is more usually with '*same* sex', not 'other sex'.

The message of the ancient story of Abraham and Sodom is clear. Hospitality offered leads to blessing. Hospitality rejected leads to destruction. The irony is that this message poses a very direct challenge in relation to the historic treatment of gay communities by the Church and society.

The biblical obligation to offer hospitality to 'outsiders' challenges the very basis on which communities presume to exclude others. A stranger, after all, is someone you cannot as yet make a judgement about. As you do not know them, the only basis for welcome is your shared humanity. Abraham honoured this principle. The obligation of hospitality confronts the behaviour of any community that excludes others to ensure the maintenance of its own closed, hierarchical, moral or social preoccupations.

Furthermore, the story makes plain that hospitality is a *theological* obligation. The refusal to welcome the 'other' into the midst is actually an assault on God's own honour who is present in the story as a guest (see Jesus' 'you did it to *me*', Matthew 25.40; my emphasis). There are also parallels here with the parable of the Good Samaritan (Luke 10.25–37). As we have already noted, there is no way of identifying the ethnicity or religious affiliation of a man who is naked and close to death before offering help. He could be *anyone*. Those who pass by at a distance do so rather than risk rendering themselves ritually unclean by touching a non-Jew or a dead body. Wherever a compassionless hierarchy of religious and moral self-preservation by-passes the obligation to love and welcome fellow humans, the gospel stands in judgement.

But such exclusion and rejection has all too often been the experience of gay people in the Church. Inclusion has come at the price of secrecy or compliance. Writing of his experience as a gay Christian in the Church, James Alison makes the same point:

We are a 'they'. Dangerous people whose most notable characteristic is not a shared humanity, but a tendency to commit acts considered to be gravely, objectively disordered. Typically our inclusion within the structure of church life comes at a very high price: that of agreeing not to speak honestly.[2]

It is good to find places where this behaviour is being challenged within churches that hold more traditional views on the subject. Living Out is a support and teaching network for gay (and therefore, in their understanding, celibate) Christians (www.livingout.org). They have been vocal in confronting churches that, while using the language of welcome, have been excluding by never actually trusting their members who are gay with ministry responsibility or leadership roles.

A few years ago, UK society was scandalized by the discovery that gangs of heterosexual men had been systematically grooming, raping and abusing young girls. The first such story surfaced in the northern town of Rotherham. Now, suppose the watching society was so scandalized by this behaviour that the name of the town entered the English language in the term 'rothering'. Although the original story concerned specific criminal behaviour, suppose that 'rothomy' and 'to rother' became a common term for referring to any sexual behaviour between heterosexuals and those with heterosexual orientation were called 'rothers'. Heterosexual people would be forever identified by this name and its originating story – with its associations with utterly abominable, antisocial and sexually abusive behaviour. Suppose that those suspected of such affections were violently persecuted and excluded. Many would simply hide their sexual orientation. Suppose that this became a legal term in many countries and those exposed as rothers faced imprisonment. Some might even campaign for the death penalty. The message of the Church would be that rothomy was the sin of sins and people needed to repent. Only celibate life was an acceptable response.

That is what the historic Church and society did when it linked the name Sodom to the life, love and relationships of folk we call 'homosexual' today. So a city that the Bible remembers for its brutal inhospitality has somehow become a byword for all that is presumed to be evil, malign and disordered about a particular expression of human desire and behaviour. The actual sin of inhospitality is replaced by a supposed sin of same-sex behaviour.

This story, and its interpretation, serves as a serious warning as to how disastrously we can and do sometimes misread the ancient Bible texts.

10

'Male and female he created them': gender, partnership and becoming

We are in the midst of far-reaching changes in our understanding of sexuality, gender and relationships in our society, and their impact is not to be minimized. We have not been here before. Many are feeling very unprepared for what this asks of our faith, our relationships and our communities.

The world my parents were born into was shaped around a firm social ordering based on gender. There was the man's world and there was the woman's world. Both had clear roles and responsibilities. A separation was apparent in all parts of life – education, career options, healthcare, home, marketplace, clothing and personal appearance.

Physical differences were presumed to reflect inner differences, such as the mental, emotional and temperamental make-up of men and women. Men were considered to be stronger and more reliable in every way. Women were the 'weaker sex', more emotional and less rational, and in need of support. Versions of these stereotypes had long been established in the history of the Church and are still found in arguments against women occupying leadership roles in it today. Boundaries are, of course, a necessary part of any social ordering. There was a practical wisdom and necessity at work, but it was also a firmly patriarchal society that prioritized and privileged men at the expense of women, in ways we remain slow to acknowledge.[1]

Over the last sixty years or so, those boundaries have been challenged. Careers and social roles that were hitherto thought to be suited only to men have been opened to women. Assumptions had been based on traditional beliefs about gender differences. At best there continues to be a challenging and creative exploration of what being men and women actually means in our time. The progress remains uneven, however. There is still a long way to go.

Partly in response to this, those holding more traditional approaches to the debate on gender, sexuality and the Bible have been moving away from a familiar focus on 'the texts'[2] that supposedly support the condemnation of same-sex relationships, the meaning and relevance of which have been under sustained challenge. Discussion is now more focused on the Genesis creation stories in considering what is presumed to be the foundational divine ordering of creation and humanity 'in the beginning'. There we read:

God created humankind in his image,
in the image of God he created them;
male and female he created them.
(Genesis 1.27)

Traditional interpretations vary but require an understanding that the first human, Adam, was a sexually undifferentiated/androgynous being whom God divided into male and female on the creation of Eve. Humanity is thus, separately, male and female. Heterosexual marriage is therefore uniquely important, for it is a literal reuniting of what was divided in the creation of Eve.

There are problems with this starting place. It is an idea more clearly found in Plato[3] than in Genesis, where no suggestion of an original undivided human is found at all. Rather, 'male and female he created *them*' (Genesis 1.27). If the first Adam had been a dual being (with, presumably, two centres of consciousness), in what sense was he alone? The Hebrew words for the first human beings are gendered (man/woman: *ish/ishah*), whereas 'Adam' is a generic word (as in 'humanity'). In Genesis 2.23, Eve is taken out of the side of the man (*ish*), not from an undifferentiated human being (*'adam*). Adam is already *male* in this story (as repeated in 1 Corinthians 11.8).

Among those holding more traditional views are those who claim that the creation story teaches a complementarity between man and woman. There are many variations of this belief, but the most common appeal is to anatomical and biological complementarity. Look at how naturally the bodies of men and women fit together, the argument goes – they are made for one another! This is regularly asserted in debates about sexuality. The *physical* complementarity of men and women's bodies is presumed to confirm the gendered ordering of human creation. Furthermore, it is claimed that the binary union of male and female together completes the image of God in humanity. Since a same-sex couple do not 'fit' in this way, it must follow that:

> homosexual behaviour . . . is a violation of the existence of male and female ordained by God in creation . . . [and] same-sex intercourse represents a suppression of the visible evidence in nature regarding male and female anatomical and procreative complementarity.[4]

The key question at this point is whether anatomical and procreative complementarity is what the Bible writers had in mind where they appear to condemn same-sex relationships elsewhere. There is no evidence for this view. Moreover, is the image of God in humanity really found expressed only through heterosexual marriage and sexual union? Logically this means that only a married man and woman are in the image of God. Single and unmarried people, or any other expressions of committed relationships, are not in God's image – or are incomplete or flawed expressions of it. This argument also comes close to implying that there is sexual differentiation within God – which is utterly foreign to the biblical tradition. By contrast Augustine and Aquinas follow the majority Christian tradition in finding the image of God expressed in humanity's unique capacity to think, reason and discern. If so, then marriage, gender and sexuality, while significant in themselves, are not relevant to discussions about divine image and likeness.

The creation texts in Genesis teach nothing more about being male and female than that it is a shared vocation to 'be fruitful and multiply' and to subdue the earth (Genesis 1.28). Likewise, in the second creation account Eve is created as a 'helper' for Adam (expressing partnership, equality and mutuality), but no more guidance is offered. Nothing is spelled out about actual gender differences. The story stresses similarity, not complementarity and difference.

We might note that no other relationships of *any* kind are found in these stories. So is heterosexual marriage the only human relationship ordered by God and of interest to him? The second story also comes embedded in the cultural assumptions of an ancient, Near Eastern, patriarchal society. It is told entirely from the male perspective and presumes a world created and ordered wholly around the man's needs. Adam is alone. God populates an entire world to assist his search for a partner, but no other creature suits him. At last woman is made for the man (but not the man for the woman). He names her. Eve has no voice, will or choice in the matter. There is no mutuality. Does this reflect our contemporary, biblical and Christian understanding of gender, marriage and relationships?

Of course, there are observable differences between men and women, but what is to be understood by these? Which, if any, of them expresses a fixed divine ordering that may vary, perhaps quite considerably, across time and culture? Though the creation stories show no interest in these questions, this has not stopped their being used as the basis for highly detailed theories as to the distinctiveness of men and women. These include the belief in a divinely intended gender hierarchy (reinforced by readings of passages in the New Testament about headship and women in subordinate roles). The claim is further made that 'Complementarity extends also to a range of personality traits and predispositions that contributes to make heterosexual unions enormously more successful in terms of fidelity, endurance, and house than same-sex ones'.[5]

There is so much to challenge here. What are these 'personality traits and predispositions' exactly? Where does the Bible discuss them? Until gay people and their relationships enjoy the same sustained support, welcome and resources that heterosexual relationships do, without the hostility, exclusion and violence they have long endured, any comparison with the presumed 'success' of heterosexual unions is meaningless.

Finally, belief in anatomical complementarity ends up with the focus of sex entirely on genital activity.[6] It also ignores any other expressions of non-coital sexual intimacy or contact, even among heterosexual couples. Are these condemned too? What we have here is an outcome of overly literal, speculative

79

interpretations of imagery found within an ancient Near Eastern poetic narrative.

Assumptions about gender roles are key to interpreting one of the core passages in the New Testament in this debate. In 1 Corinthians 6.9, Paul lists ten behaviours that exclude people from the kingdom of God. It includes adulterers, thieves, the greedy and drunkards, and describes forms of unjust, indulgent or abusive behaviour. Two words on the list – the Greek words *arsenokoitai* and *malakoi* – are less straightforward to understand. In English Bibles, they are commonly assumed to belong together, though, as we have noted, no other words in this list are paired.

The meaning of *arsenokoitai* cannot be certain because the word appears nowhere else in any Greek literature. This strongly suggests that it was a local coinage, originating in the Jewish cultural context. It seems most likely that, in using this word, Paul has in mind the prohibitions in Leviticus 18.22 that I discussed in Chapter 5, but we are told no more. So what activity does the word describe and why is it condemned? It is important to realize that in the Greek and Roman culture of Paul's day, sexuality was understood in terms of an *action*, not an orientation. To be the active/dominant partner in sex (with *anyone*) was to be virile and manly, and it was the right of every free man. To be the passive partner was to be weak and effeminate.[7] *Arsenokoitai* therefore seems to refer to the dominant male bed partner in male–male sexual intercourse. However, the word can be understood only within the cultural assumptions of the time, where it most likely carried connotations of slavery, idolatry and social dominance which typified that ancient society. That would make sense of its being included in Paul's list of condemnations here.

Malakoi literally means 'soft', 'fine'. Jesus uses the word when speaking to his followers about John the Baptist: 'What then did you go out to see? Someone dressed in soft robes?' (Matthew 11.8). Some therefore believe that the word here refers to excessive, wealthy self-indulgence. That would fit the tone of the rest of the list.

Many English Bibles translate *malakoi* as 'effeminate'. Effeminate is a derogatory term used of men who are behaving in ways more typically associated with, or expected of, 'women' – that is, being 'unmanly'. The term has meaning only in a social context where there are specific requirements of role behaviour between the sexes – and specifically *male* roles. In Paul's list of abusive and unjust behaviours that exclude people from the kingdom of God, being 'effeminate' or 'unmanly' sits oddly. What is the relevance today, theologically and socially, of judging sexual intercourse in terms of active and passive roles? Does this really result in exclusion from the kingdom of God?

But Paul is not judging *any* sex. The context is specific, though not immediately accessible to contemporary readers of a translated text. His condemnation is aimed specifically at coercive and abusive behaviour of various kinds: 'Paul is thinking of practices which do injury to others and will be recognized as such by his readers. That is, he does not condemn these practices as homosexual, but as unloving and harmful.'[8]

So what does it mean to be a man or a woman? Do we even fully know yet? That is not to say the idea of gender is now irrelevant or neutral. It is not, but nor is it for narrowly defining in ways that are familiar through church and social history. Instead of looking back to find a supposed and possibly imaginary fixed ordering in the beginning, we would be on sounder ground accepting that we are on a journey of exploration into something new. If we could do that, the Christian faith might become a place of faithful exploration and wisdom as we seek the good of an emerging society and culture in confusing times, rather than presenting a defensive and reactive face to the world that is too commonly associated with it.

To be a woman or a man is still God-given, as in the beginning. It is a source of wonder, challenge, creativity and mystery, and is full of possibility. To be a man or woman is no one thing. There has always been a spectrum of self-understanding and expression. What we have in common is the call to authentic love, living, giving and belonging. Each of us must travel our own path and accept particular gifts and challenges on the way. The stories we hear of gender transition warn us of the danger of assuming that someone's identity is defined solely by the physical body. Though the call to parent and care for children will always find a unique expression in heterosexual union, it now needs to be part of a more extended discussion. It has also long been the case that alternative expressions of parenting have been lovingly offered where children would otherwise be left without secure attachment at all. The consistent evidence is that children brought up in homes with same-sex couples flourish and achieve no less than those in homes with male and female parents.[9]

The Archbishop of Canterbury expressed the challenge facing all Christian communities in our times when he called for:

a radical new Christian inclusion in the Church . . . founded in Scripture, in reason, in tradition, in theology . . . based on good, healthy, flourishing relationships, and in a proper twenty-first-century understanding of being human and of being sexual.[10]

11

One flesh:
Genesis, kinship and marriage

Even for those who have come to accept same-sex partnerships, the question of whether such relationships can or should be called 'marriage' often remains an uncertainty. That marriage is a covenant between a man and a woman has been, until very recently, unquestioned. The extension of marriage to same-sex couples is without precedent in history. For some it marks the final departure from the biblical creation ordering, declared 'good' by God in the beginning.

The appeal to history is often made: 'The Church has taught this for 2,000 years.' Something that is widely believed, and for a very long time, is not to be changed lightly, but longevity is not in itself a guarantee of truth: it is just something that we have believed for a very long time. Pioneering biologists and cosmologists (among others) know well how fiercely new evidence questioning established beliefs is (initially) opposed on religious grounds. If we are unwilling or unable to imagine the possibility of new ways of knowing in our world, however, we will be unable to respond faithfully to the questions that this unfolding world is always posing.

In fact, it is simply not true that one understanding of marriage has been taught throughout history. The appeal to 'biblical' marriage is not a straightforward one either. The range of possibilities has included polygamy (more than one wife or concubine, simultaneously); partnerships beyond marriage for the man (since the man can have access to the female slaves or servants in the house); the obligation of a rapist to marry his victim (Deuteronomy 22.28–29); levirate marriage (the obligation of the brother of the deceased husband to marry the childless widow (see Deuteronomy 23.5–10); and monogamy. The woman in all this is owned, a form of property. Thus Ruth becomes Boaz's wife only as an add-on to a land purchase deal that another relative backs out of (Ruth chapters 3–4).

Many marriage practices in the Bible are no longer practised or even considered acceptable by the Church, while features of contemporary expressions of marriage are not found in the Bible at all. Furthermore, the most prominent church leader in the New Testament urged Christians to remain single, like him (1 Corinthians 7.9) – a teaching that churches today ignore, in my experience!

This means that those defending a 'traditional' institution of marriage from history need to make clear which expression of marriage they are arguing for and what they are basing their case on. Throughout history, marriage has always been a flexible and evolving social and religious institution. So there is a contradiction when the conservative Evangelical corner of the Church of England, while insisting that there is one traditional, historic view of marriage taught in the Bible, asks for its own bishop to support – among other issues – its belief that the Bible teaches an ordering of human relationships and marriage based on gender subordination and complementarianism.[1] As this has never been the 'traditional' teaching of the Church from Scripture, it is immediately apparent that more than one view of marriage presently exists within the Evangelical tradition alone.

Another challenge to claims of a uniform historic church teaching was illustrated by the controversy sparked by the invitation of spouses to the Lambeth Conference of Bishops in 2020. This raised a problem because two such couples (at the time) were in same-sex marriages. To invite them would have risked a major boycott by bishops holding more traditional views on this subject. The official statement claimed that the decision not to invite them was on the basis of 'the Anglican Communion's position on marriage which is that it is the lifelong union of a man and a woman'.[2] That this is clearly *not* the present Anglican teaching on marriage is clear from the fact that a number of invited bishops (and/or their spouses) had divorced and remarried. If 'lifelong union' is the Church's understanding of marriage, they should not have been invited either.

The creation account in Genesis 2 is seen as foundational for the Christian debate about same-sex marriage. Surely God has revealed there his intention for marriage 'in the beginning'. So how do Christians read this account? Do those texts warn against or forbid the extending of marriage beyond the union of a man and a woman?

In that poetic narrative, the first human being is formed from the dust and given life in God's good creation – but he is alone. God provides a partner for him. The mutual joy and partnership of the man and woman, imaging God, in marriage affirms God's created intention for humanity. They are literally made for one another. Surely, then, the argument goes, marriage is for male and female. So much seems self-evident.

It seems obvious to point out that any account of the origins of humanity will, *of necessity*, be a telling of the creation and union of a man and women. It is not only the Hebrew and Christian traditions that have therefore created forms of public covenant for this relationship to ensure its honouring and protection in society. That is as it should be. As already noted in the previous chapter, this creation account shows no interest in any details of gender differences or roles and, as we shall see, it is *similarity*, not difference, that is stressed here. Nothing beyond that is decreed.

The Church of England wedding service calls marriage 'a gift of God in creation', but marriage is not actually found in the Genesis account itself. After Adam's joyful recognition of Eve, God did not create an institution called 'marriage'. No legal or religious ceremony took place. No promises were exchanged. That we are to find in this ancient story the origins of what we call 'marriage' is made clear only in an aside by the narrator. After Adam has chosen Eve as his suitable helper, the narrator comments, 'Therefore a man leaves his father and his mother and clings to his wife, and they become one flesh' (Genesis 2.24). This means that, in the narrator's world, something called marriage already exists, but all we know about it in this text is the 'at last' moment of recognition and choice by Adam followed by three actions – leaving, clinging and becoming one flesh (told exclusively, we may note, from the perspective of the man and his needs).

So what is 'one flesh'? This is commonly assumed to be expressing the sexual union of the man and woman in marriage. It works well as a poetic image of the intimacy of lovemaking, but nowhere in the Bible does 'one flesh' refer to sexual love. The Hebrew word (*basar*) means 'relatives'. 'One flesh' actually means 'one kinship group'. An example is Laban's exclamation when he meets his relative Jacob – 'you are my bone and my flesh!' (Genesis 29.14; see also 2 Samuel 5.1). Here is the context of the otherwise strange reference to the man leaving his parents – for in that ancient world it was the woman who left her home to marry, not the man. This is emphasizing the central place of marriage in the reshaping and renewing of primary kinship groups: 'The focus is not on sexual union but on the formation of the essential and foundational building blocks of human community.'[3] This is not to diminish the importance of marriage for the couple, but their union forms part of a much wider context of belonging. Christian readings of this story regularly miss the significance of this.

The context of Jesus' teaching on divorce is also found here. When he refers back to this verse and to becoming 'one flesh' he is making a statement about the utterly destructive effect of divorce on the whole fabric of the community (for example, Matthew 19.1–12). The text is not concerned with *who* can marry. Jesus is making a wider point about the importance of kinship.

What if we take a step back and ask, 'Why were human beings created in the first place?' The answer given in Genesis 2 is to till the ground (v. 15). The story begins with the earth barren for lack of rain and the lack of someone to care for and work it. Adam ('earth creature') is formed. Creation begins to flourish through God's gift and Adam's care. Adam's need for a helper is therefore much more than an emotional or sexual need. Brownson is correct to warn us 'not to overgenitalize or oversexualize this passage'.[4] Nor is the focus here on romantic, privatized ideas of personal fulfilment. Adam is alone, not lonely. He is incomplete for the task he has been made for. He needs a helper – someone with whom to share the work. This too is part of the image and work of kinship. The aloneness of Adam surely includes longings for intimacy and relationship but, once again, the focus is wider. He cannot do all this on his own. 'One flesh' expresses loving mutuality, partnership and shared vocation on the earth.

'Clinging' also expresses this multilayered commitment. An example is found in the moving moment where Ruth 'clung' to her mother-in-law Naomi and refuses to leave her (Ruth 1.14). It is the same word used in Genesis 2.24 and this is surely deliberate – but not because Ruth's clinging is sexual. This is about kinship. By the end of the story, Ruth's determined, loving clinging has enabled an extraordinary new kinship, out of despair and exile, and across race, culture and religion. For this she is celebrated as a matriarch alongside the patriarch Abraham (Ruth 4.11).

Back in the creation story, Adam is alone. Where is a suitable helper to be found? In the first creation account, when something was needed God simply decreed it and it happened. Here in the second story, in the search for a helper or companion, the choice is left to the human being. God decrees nothing (except what is *not* good – Adam is alone); rather, he is present as one who serves (see Jesus in Luke 22.27), creating creature after creature in the search for a suitable helper for Adam. The narrator presents this as a genuine search though the scene is not without comic potential. Only Adam, it seems, can recognize who is suitable. He must choose – but what is he looking for?

Perhaps the clearest summary in that ancient world of what Adam was seeking is found in the tribute to the 'valorous wife' in the last chapter of the book of Proverbs.[5] Subverting familiar patriarchal assumptions (that even the creation story does not avoid), the helpmate's life and gifts are celebrated in the language of fulsome praise and grateful mutuality. She is portrayed as the image of Lady Wisdom herself. The list of her achievements is long and varied but, surprisingly, without any mention of fertility, childbearing or motherhood. Children appear, but only near the end where they add their praises to the final doxology (Proverbs 31.28).

Meanwhile, God finally creates woman *from within* and *out of* the man. Eve is recognized and celebrated. Here is more than a work colleague. She is plainly a delight to him! Gareth Moore spells out the significance of this:

A companion, in the sense of companionship which is in view in this text, is somebody you actually want to be with and share your life with. An imposed companion would be no companion at all. There is no divine blueprint; there is only what makes glad the heart of each of us.[6]

Here contemporary practice finds resonance with the ancient text. It is the couple who make a marriage, not the Church. The couple minister the sacrament of marriage to one another. The Church witnesses and blesses what has *already been chosen*.

It is often argued that a same-sex partnership cannot be a marriage because, in the words of one writer, it is 'intrinsically closed to procreation'.[7] Logically this means that heterosexual unions which do not produce children cannot be marriages either. In fact, the creation account in Genesis 2 nowhere links marriage to procreation, nor is procreation found as a marriage requirement anywhere else in the Bible. So the Book of Common Prayer marriage service is simply wrong when it states that marriage was 'First . . . ordained for the procreation of children'.[8] Furthermore, although having children is the hope and intention of many couples entering marriage, the Bible nowhere defines marriage by its capacity to be a sexually procreative union. With the exception of the Roman Catholic Church, marriage is open to couples whose union will not, for a variety of reasons, be procreative.

In the light of all this, is it any clearer why marriage must be confined to a man and a woman? It is true that there are no examples of same-sex marriages in the Bible. Nor is there a hint of a trajectory in that direction. But what we are living with in our times is so significantly new that there are limits to how much we will be helped by looking back. Rather than focusing on supposed origins, we should recognize that Christian marriage, like all discipleship, is significant for what it points towards. We have in our midst an important community of fellow Christians who simply do not recognize themselves, or their vocation to love and partnership, in those ancient texts. What, then, is the objection to opening marriage to couples of the same sex whose union will not conceive children but who have recognized one another in love and so would leave, cling and become one flesh?

Oliver O'Donovan writes:

> the world has never seen a phenomenon like the contemporary gay consciousness. There have been various patterns of homosexuality in various cultures, but none with the constellation of features and persistent self-assertion that this one presents. And we need hardly be surprised at this turn in history if we reflect on the extraordinary discontinuities that exist between late modern society, and ancient societies. To live in our time, as in any other, is to have a unique set of practical questions to address.[9]

A core question to be explored is: 'What is there in the vocation to one-flesh kinship that a same-sex couple cannot uniquely express and fulfil?' Given the divinely willed place of choice in this story, why can the joyful exclamation – 'at last . . . bone of my bones' (Genesis 2.23) – not also be the delighted recognition of someone of the *same* sex?

We are trying to work through the challenge of how a deeply rooted traditional institution, and the communities it is found within, may adapt themselves to contemporary expressions of committed social and sexual relating. Historically there is nothing new in this task, but the change has been so rapid that the Church has been left trying to catch up in its thinking and practice. As I write, questions about trans identity are taking centre stage, while the debates about marriage remain unresolved and deeply conflicted in the Church.

One writer suggests that this simply comes down to whether we believe that two people of the same sex can actually love one another:

> I don't mean desire or be attracted or enjoy good times together. I mean love – self-giving, care providing, bloody-minded, doggedly faithful love. If the answer is 'yes' then there is only the question of how that love can be supported and disciplined (or discipled).[10]

This would not require a change to the doctrine of marriage. It simply explores the extending of this vocation to couples of the same sex. Nor need heterosexual marriage feel under threat or undermined by this. The union of husband and wife continues to be a metaphor of extraordinary intimacy for expressing the love of Christ for his Church and the joyful fullness that is life in God. It must always and everywhere be 'a way of life that all should honour'. It is for this reason that some who support committed same-sex relationships seek another name for it – such as covenant friendship.[11] I understand the concern, for Christian marriage expresses so much more than the issue of equality and 'rights', which too easily takes over this debate. The challenge to those of us arguing for the extension of marriage in the Church is to also extend the theological and sacramental richness of what marriage expresses in the New Testament. In this way marriage need not be an exclusive metaphor. It becomes a glorious and unique expression of the vocation to love and belong that all humanity shares and expresses.

Marriage in the Bible is a vocation expressed in terms of recognition, choice, leaving and clinging, kinship and as a means to work for the care of creation. Is there any reason why it should not include those who have found delight, blessing and divine gift in someone of the same sex?

12

Call nothing unclean: the vision beyond the text

The first Christians were Jewish believers. They continued to worship as Jews in the Temple or in the synagogues until they were finally excluded and had to form their own churches. They continued to practise circumcision and obey the ritual, purity and dietary laws of their Hebrew faith. This also required them to practise strict separation from non-Jews. A turning point came when these fledgling churches began to accept 'outsiders' into full membership and took their first divisive steps towards being a church for all. Though this did not happen in one single place and time, it is remembered through one particular story.

The story of Peter's dream at Joppa is relevant in the context of this book for two particular reasons. It tells of how the first Jewish churches came to include those who had historically been excluded as unclean. For this to happen, Christian insiders had to disobey their own Scriptures. Rather than outsiders becoming 'clean', believers had to make themselves *unclean*. This is a story within the Bible that faithfully goes *beyond* the Bible.

The apostle Peter is lodging in a house at the seaport of Joppa. His host, a fellow Jew, is a tanner by trade. This in itself raises questions. Handling carcasses rendered Jewish tanners almost permanently unclean. Simon would have been excluded from worshipping with his own community without repeatedly going through lengthy purity rituals. In this curious way the central issue of the story is introduced (Acts 10.1–11.18).

We meet Peter praying on the roof and waiting for food to eat. He has a vision. It has a dream-like quality and dreams are often hard to relate on waking. This one is no exception. We can imagine him trying: 'Well, there was a sail cloth – but it wasn't on a boat. It came down from heaven like a sort of large basket.' Most translators opt for 'sheet' but 'sail cloth' is just as possible and surely more likely. This is often how dream/trance imagery works – familiar things appear in unfamiliar places doing strange things. Peter is a professional sailor, on a housetop at a busy seaport. Sails are part of his trade. He is hungry and he has been praying. A sail comes down to him, from heaven, as a large food parcel.

But the vision sounds more like a nightmare. The container is teeming with food that orthodox Jews were expressly forbidden to eat by the Bible. A voice says, 'Get up, Peter; kill and eat' (v. 13). Peter rightly protests that he cannot. The voice replies, 'What God has made clean, you must not call profane' (v. 15). This happens three times. The vision fades. As he tries to make sense of it, messengers arrive at the front door below. He is asked to go with them to the house of an (unclean) Gentile believer in Caesarea.

So for the first time in his life, along with six other Jewish believers, Peter enters the house of a Gentile. Cornelius was a God-fearing Gentile – a term for non-Jews who had attached themselves to the Jewish faith but were not circumcised or living under the Jewish law as Jews did. They were devout outsiders. They could never be fully included at the heart of Jewish faith and were kept separate when attending worship. Cornelius is spoken of, we are told, with great respect.

Peter tells Cornelius that a Jew should not be entering his house and associating with him and his family, but that God had told him 'I should not call anyone . . . unclean' (Acts 10.28). There is no overestimating what an enormous step this would have been for Peter and his group. Cornelius, in turn, tells of his vision and Peter is moved to declare, 'I truly understand that God shows no partiality' (10.34) and begins to preach. The Spirit interrupts Peter's sermon, falling dramatically on the Gentile household: 'The circumcised believers who had come with Peter were astounded that the gift of the Holy Spirit had been poured out *even on the Gentiles*' (10.45; my emphasis). Those last words reveal just how exclusive the first believers still presumed their faith and church to be.

Not surprisingly, news of all this spreads fast. Peter is summoned to Jerusalem to explain himself. 'The circumcised believers' (already identified here with a particular voice within the Church) confront him for entering and eating in a Gentile house (Acts 11.3). Peter's response is to simply tell what happened. The community of Jerusalem accept his testimony (Acts 11.4–8). No theological discussion is reported here. The contradiction between Peter's testimony and the unambiguous Bible teachings on exclusion and separation is simply not addressed. The first Christians disobey Scripture to obey God.

We now hear of something similar happening in Antioch. Other Christians had been sharing their faith across the region but only with fellow Jews, but some in Antioch began sharing the gospel with Gentiles, who were being converted in large numbers. This causes deep divisions between the 'circumcised believers' and the Gentile believers. A council is called at Jerusalem to thrash this out (Acts 15). They debate at length. Peter is now supported by Paul and Barnabas (who had been cheerfully continuing to convert Gentiles en route to the meeting!) Their testimony, again, is compelling. It is agreed that

only two requirements should be laid on Gentile believers –
to abstain from eating meat offered to idols and from fornica-
tion. The reasons for prioritizing these two are not completely
obvious and are not explained. Paul himself proceeded to
ignore the first.

There are a number of things to notice in this extraordinary
story.

- The meeting that so radically transformed the early Church's
  life and mission begins with the faith and prayer of a separated
  outsider.
- This means that, instead of being the presumed centre of
  God's mission, the Church found itself on the *outside* of the
  God story, needing to listen, watch, learn and obey. Instead
  of being a church welcoming others *in*, it found itself being
  invited in by those on the outside. Not all could make this
  journey, and some strongly opposed it. This warns us that the
  Church can find itself struggling with, and even opposing,
  the wider vision of what God is doing.
- In the earliest days of its life and mission, the Christian
  Church found itself responding to situations that challenged
  or even contradicted received tradition and teaching.
- The story gives central place to experience and testimony. By
  contrast, the appeal to testimony and personal experiences
  is often treated with suspicion today. It is asserted that
  the Bible must judge experience, not the other way round.
  I would claim that I experienced Christ and the life of the
  Spirit among friends who happened to be gay before I had
  worked out my theology on human sexuality. That is true for
  many. If the Bible challenges and interprets our experience
  (as it rightly does), Peter's story tells us there are times when

our experience will challenge how we read and understand the Bible.

- One of the puzzles is the lack of Scripture in this story. Peter hears a voice telling him to eat food forbidden in the Torah, and to call nothing unclean. On the basis of this vision he enters the house of an 'unclean' Gentile and sees the Spirit of God fall on outsiders. Where can he go in the Bible to understand this? Something very different is going on. There is a familiar challenge posed to those who support the inclusion of gay people in the Church: 'You can't show one Bible text to support this.' But could Peter and the first Christians have done so either? Now, there *are* texts in the Hebrew Scriptures that speak of the inclusion of the Gentiles. Israel is to be 'a light to the nations, that my salvation may reach to the end of the earth' (Isaiah 49.6). God speaks to non-Israelite nations through the prophet Hosea saying, 'I will say to Not My People, "You are my people"' (Hosea 2.23). Simply quoting such verses is misleading, however. Though these prophecies foresee Gentiles welcomed into the Jewish world and religion, it is *on Jewish terms*. That is why so much of the argument about Gentile believers in the New Testament centred around how *Jewish* they needed to be – the food they ate, whether they were required to be circumcised, keeping the law, and so on. By contrast, what began at Cornelius's house was a vision of altogether greater inclusion. Scripture is pointing beyond Scripture.

This was a vision that the New Testament Church initially received as disturbing and contradictory through the subverting work of the Spirit. It was the vision of a new community, based on a radically new belonging and identity in Christ. It was yet to be fully revealed and was based on no familiar divisions of race, gender or social class: 'There is no longer Jew or Greek, there is no longer slave or free, there is no longer male and female; for all of you are one in Christ Jesus' (Galatians 3.28).

This story is not included here because it says anything about sexuality. It doesn't, but it is an example, from the first Christian churches, of a vulnerable stepping out in faith, into something very new, shocking, even unthinkable. It presents the challenge of responding obediently to what feels to be the inspiration of the Spirit even though it appears to contradict the plainest traditional understandings of the given texts. For me, that illustrates something of the challenge facing the Church today in relation to issues of sexuality and gay relationships.

We should not be surprised that gay Christians find many parallels in this story of divinely initiated inclusion of devout but excluded outsiders into the Church – and of sustained resistance to their growing presence. James Alison is a Roman Catholic Christian who is also gay:

This has been exactly our experience as LGBT Catholics over the last thirty or so years. It has become clearer and clearer, until it is now overwhelmingly clear, that what used to seem like a self-evident description of us was in fact mistaken. We were characterized as somehow defective, pathological, or vitiated straight people; intrinsically heterosexual people who were suffering from a bizarre and extreme form of heterosexual concupiscence called 'same-sex attraction'. That description, which turned us, in practice, into second-class citizens in God's house, is quite simply false.[1]

The final message of this story is one we are all too aware of. Becoming a truly including community, under the compelling work of the Spirit, is a long, divisive and painful process.

The Jewish–Gentile tension runs unresolved through the whole New Testament Church. Traditional pressure groups (called Judaizers) were travelling around lobbying local congregations, violently opposed to Paul's teaching and doing all they could to oppose it. Then, as now, feelings ran high on all sides. Paul himself exploded with frustration more than once: 'Why don't these agitators, obsessive as they are about circumcision, go all the way and castrate themselves!' (Galatians 5.12 MSG).

The Jewish/Gentile division was surely the early Church's version of our sexuality debates. Perhaps they too wondered if 'good disagreement' was even possible.

13

Good fruit:
patience, trust and the test of time

Those speaking and writing in support of same-sex relationships are often accused of being false teachers by people holding different views. Now it is certainly very important to be able to tell the difference between what is true and what is false. The issue was a continuing concern in the New Testament churches. On one occasion, Jesus himself warned his followers to 'Beware of false prophets'. Such people come in disguise, he says: they look like sheep but are actually wolves (Matthew 7.15). So how were they to tell the difference?

Jesus did not set biblical or doctrinal tests for measuring orthodoxy. What he offered was an altogether more practical way to tell:

> You will know them by their fruits. Are grapes gathered from thorns, or figs from thistles? In the same way, every good tree bears good fruit, but the bad tree bears bad fruit. A good tree cannot bear bad fruit, nor can a bad tree bear good fruit. (Matthew 7.16–18)

So in the face of a situation the gift (or threat) of which is not immediately apparent, Jesus offered his Church a way of proceeding that might be called godly pragmatism.

The test of fruit proceeds in a variety of ways. It takes seriously the positive contribution of lived experience. The Archbishop of Canterbury gave a striking example of this when he said, 'You see gay relationships that are just stunning in the quality of the relationship.' He made clear that he was speaking of 'particular friends where I recognise that and am deeply challenged by it'.[1]

Fruit needs time to grow and reveal its quality. In fact, like all growth, it begins out of sight – so this must be a longer-term discernment strategy. It requires of us a willingness to wait. It needs the virtue of patience and a trusting relationship in terms of both time and outcomes. It also asks for the capacity to live with unresolved questions and, possibly, with evidence that appears to contradict our received beliefs.

The test of fruit cannot be based on prior assumptions about what is good or bad. The fruit is allowed to speak for itself. The process is for trusting. 'Nor can a bad tree bear good fruit' (Matthew 7.18), says Jesus.

As fruit needs tending and care for it to grow at all, the test of fruit requires a hands-on commitment to loving, hospitable, non-anxious inclusion. Discernment cannot happen at a 'safe' distance. We must taste and see.

When the fruit we are testing is new or 'other' to us, particular care is needed. Can we be sure we will recognize the good fruit when we see it? Jesus warns us against judging those who don't fit our agenda or expectations. On one occasion, his disciples tried to stop someone ministering because 'he was not following us'. He rebuked them: 'Whoever is not against us is for us' (Mark 9.38, 40).

Those following Jesus were repeatedly scandalized by where, and among whom, the fruit of his ministry and preaching took root and flourished. The evidence before their eyes did not fit their social and religious expectations. Surely you do not get such good fruit from such disreputable, bad 'trees'? The sense of scandal only deepened when Jesus called 'bad' the religious fruit of his day.

The challenge for Jesus' hearers was to recognize and accept the good fruit of the kingdom where it was now appearing, but that meant encountering faith in strange places and among very unexpected people. Perhaps a similar challenge faces the Church today? And what if this strange fruit is not to our taste or preference? We may never have come across it before. Is it even edible? But of what relevance is that to the kingdom of God?

Contemporary discussions and encounters are raising new and complex questions about sexuality and identity. The Church is not yet clear, and is often very conflicted, in its response. Something new is going on. We are on a journey that requires trust, faith and meeting beyond familiar boundaries and definitions.

I recall a conversation with a man in South Africa who, as a young man, was the first black priest to be appointed to the staff of a city centre Anglican church at the height of the apartheid era. Week by week he watched as some white worshippers crossed the aisle to avoid receiving Communion from him or left by a side door so as not to have to greet him. But he was a man of gracious faith. He absorbed the hurts and continued to offer his ministry in the face of silent hostility and opposition. Slowly things began to change. Some began to seek him out, apologizing in tears for the way that they had been treating him: 'I simply had no way of coping – of recognizing you, your faith, your ministry.'

Such stories can be repeated where people have received and come to welcome the good fruit of the ministry of women, having previously opposed that fundamental change. They are repeated where the good fruit of the lives of Christian men and women who happen to be gay can no longer be denied and are now welcomed.

When a friend was invited to lead a group of Christian ministers in a discussion about 'homosexuality', he startled them by suggesting that those in the room who were heterosexual might begin by sharing their sexual desires and relationships. The point he was making very effectively is that this is how many debates about same-sex sexuality and relationships tend to proceed. The lifestyles and sexual preferences of gay people, their capacity (or incapacity) to form and sustain relationships, are publicly discussed, scrutinized and statistically analysed. It is about *them* – whether *they* are good or bad fruit. Where this proceeds from a prior conviction that such people *cannot* be good fruit, a particular potential to do harm is evident. Heterosexual men and women, no matter how good, bad or indifferent the quality of their sexual life and relationships, have no experience of what this treatment is like.

I confess, I do not have difficulty forming opinions about other people. What is far harder to be aware of is the fruit of *my* presence on the lives of others. Do my faith and life enable a fruitful flourishing among those called, like me, to gospel faithfulness and obedience? How would I know? It has been rightly said that the last thing we discover about ourselves is our effect. Only others can tell us how they find us. So we need to listen carefully.

One of the most telling moments at a day conference on marriage and sexuality was when one of the speakers described the experience, as a gay person, of going to a new church. She spoke of how gay men and women will have learnt from long experience that they cannot be sure of a welcome. They do not

know whether this would be a safe place for them if they became identified by their sexuality. So they will be constantly
searching for clues – the notice board, the activities on the
notice sheet, the words of welcome from the front, the sermon
themes and the content of the intercessions. Words of warm
welcome may be everywhere. Sexuality may not be mentioned
at all, but the vital question may be left unanswered. That is
the problem. As a general rule, unless people hear themselves
explicitly welcomed – especially those who have good reason
to feel uncertain – they will tend to assume the opposite. The
price of belonging will then be at the cost of personal secrecy,
concealment and isolation. Churches can be bad fruit without
being aware of how or why.

As churches work through their response to the presence of
same-sex relationships, some bad fruit is unmistakable – open
hostility, bigotry, violence, exclusion and prejudice. However,
a certain kind of silence is possibly more commonly the way
churches try to manage the unsettling and divisive questions of
human sexuality.

Lizzie belonged to a lively, loving church community and had
a deep personal faith, but no one knew that she was struggling
with the knowledge that she was gay. She was unable to believe
God could possibly love her. On 10 September 2014 she took her
own life. The way her devastated church community embarked
on a journey of self-examination and change in the light of her
story is well known.[2] Lizzie's church would have described itself
as loving, open and welcoming, but it had not openly discussed
the subject of sexuality. The vicar, Nick Bundock, recalls:

I felt, wrongly, it was better not to stir up a hornet's nest
about sexuality. If we don't talk about it, people can have

their progressive or traditional views and that's fine and we won't do anything to upset the apple cart. So we won't talk about it.

This is a common response to a very divisive issue (though it needs to be said that there are not just two possible views on this issue). Bundock went on to say:

It was only later, at the coroner's hearing, that we discovered that, actually, it had been our conspiracy of silence, as it were, around the issue of sexuality, that had been the crucible in which Lizzie had existed in those months up until her death.

The church responded by drawing up a statement of inclusion. Not all could support this and some left, but out of this tragedy some unexpected fruit has been growing. Others have joined. Not only LGBTI folk but people of different races and people with disabilities have found themselves welcomed in this vision of inclusion.[3]

In 2017, the Archbishops of Canterbury and York called for 'a radical new Christian inclusion in the Church. This must be founded in scripture, in reason, in tradition, in theology and the Christian faith as the Church of England has received it.'[4] In 2018 a letter from some bishops urged that 'remaining silent on these issues is not serving the Church well'.[5]

Churches with a genuine conviction that same-sex relationships cannot be supported by Scripture face a particular challenge as to how they communicate this in their communities. More recently, churches that do not agree with women in leadership in churches have been challenged to be more publicly transparent and honest about their position. Something similar is needed in relation to sexuality.

All the cups of tea in the world won't change the hurt and the sense of vilification that comes from a version of Christianity that while outwardly using the language of welcome in fact condemns gay people's most intimate and preciously expressed love, their gentle interactions with their partners, their sweet tenderness, and shared union. If a church holds these views, gay and lesbian people will feel it. They do.[6]

What will be the marks of a community that is enabling good fruit to grow and flourish? As they seek to be places where people know themselves to be loved, accepted and listened to on their journey with Christ, their life will be marked by:

- a celebrating and reverencing of our shared gift of humanity;
- a sensitive awareness of our mutual vulnerability;
- a compassion for those who struggle and seek justice;
- a discernment of the reality of sin and evil;
- a prayer for holiness of life;
- a capacity to live honestly and openly with difference;
- a capacity to live with honest disagreement;
- grace to be gifts towards one another's fulfilling in Christ;
- truth, forgiveness, reconciliation in facing up to what is disordered and destructive in our lifestyles;
- support in seeking holiness and sustaining new patterns of living and loving.

Faithful following of Christ bears good fruit. It is the fruit of faithful, consecrated lives. It is marked by a quality of life and spirit – 'love, joy, peace, patience, kindness, generosity, faithfulness, gentleness, and self-control. There is no law against such things' (Galatians 5.22–23). This is not fruit a bad tree can produce.

14

To whom it is given: sexual abstinence and celibacy

For those who are convinced that the Bible forbids same-sex sexual partnerships or marriage, singleness and sexual abstinence is the only alternative. There is only one passage in the New Testament that discusses this kind of situation at a practical level. It comes in Paul's first letter to the church in Corinth, in which he works through a number of questions that they have put to him. It seems that, in the fervour of their faith, as they seek to follow Christ in the life of the Spirit, some believers were urging sexual abstinence and renouncing marriage, and some married couples were withdrawing from sexual relationships with one another. The church was asking Paul for guidance.

It is important to set this correspondence in its original context. The first Christians believed that they were living at the end of the age. What mattered above all else was to be ready. Didn't Jesus himself warn of the need for this (for example, Matthew 24.37–39)? 'The priority for all relationships is not whether I am single or married, gay or straight, it is whether I am living in the expectation of God's coming Kingdom.'[1]

Paul agrees with them. There is a clear urgency to his words. He urges a radical reappraisal of earthly ties, for 'the appointed time has grown short; from now on, let even those who have wives be as those who had none' (1 Corinthians 7.29). Everything must be prioritized in the light of what he calls the 'impending crisis' (7.26). So the decision to forsake marriage and the commitment to sexual abstinence in the early Church was for a very specific reason: it was 'an emergency measure enabling the Christians to concentrate on God, who will very soon bring the world to an end'.[2] After all, what long-term arrangements of *any* kind are appropriate when the consummation of the cosmos could take place tomorrow?

This is an early example of the tension between marriage and celibacy that runs unevenly through a great deal of Christian history. For long periods, celibacy was prized as a more spiritual way in the service of Christ (and still is in parts of the Church). Sex, and the passions that went with it, were seen as inherently sinful. Marriage was therefore a second-best calling (though obviously necessary for the continuation of the human race). Arguably, it is marriage that is more highly valued than celibacy today. Within and outside the Roman Catholic Church, for example, there is growing criticism of the idea of compulsory celibacy for its priests. In our wider society, the idea of living without sex is simply baffling.

Back in Corinth, Paul urges his followers to choose singleness as he has done (1 Corinthians 7). His reasons are wholly positive. He wants them to live with 'unhindered devotion to the LORD' (7.35). Marriage and family are demanding and potentially distracting. So, he advises, if you are free from such commitments, do not seek them out. It is important to point out that the choice of singleness and celibacy was envisaged as a short-term commitment in a world teetering on the brink of the coming kingdom. This means that nowhere is the concept of long-term or lifelong abstinence addressed at all in the New Testament. They were simply not expecting to be around that long.

Nevertheless, from the earliest days of the Church, significant numbers of Christians have been drawn to different expressions of consecrated single living. For some, it was within forms of monastic community and shared life. For others, it was a call to solitary prayer or a particular way of service that needed their whole commitment. Singleness was something I wondered if I was being called to at a time of deepening faith in my early adult years, but I remember how hard it was to explore this at the time, within an Evangelical tradition that had little positive understanding of it. During that time I was regularly asked to speak on singleness, and the experience underlined how little it was actually understood or valued as a vocation. In fact, the focus was strongly marriage-centred, which often resulted in a rather anxious mistrust of single people.

My observation is that churches across all traditions face the challenge of being better at understanding and honouring faithful singleness and celibacy where it is authentically found in the community. In the midst of a society so deeply damaged in its search for love and belonging, an authentic single vocation can be a liberating gift. It is a way of witnessing to the kingdom, but it may also be a witness to the freedom in life in general, including one not narrowed by an unhelpful preoccupation with sexual desire. For some, this witness may come as an immense relief.

For all his positive enthusiasm for the single state, Paul recognizes that it is not possible or right for everyone. So his pastoral advice develops in a very significant direction. Paul passes no judgement on those whose natural desires are too strong to manage. There is no hint that abstinence is better than sex. His response to an unnamed believer who is struggling with sexual desire is: 'if his passions are strong, and so it has to be, let him marry as he wishes; it is no sin' (1 Corinthians 7.36). (Paul writes mainly to men in this passage.) It is no failure, sin or weakness to be unable to manage without the expression of sexual desire. Paul is quite pragmatic about that: 'it is better to marry than to be aflame with passion' (7.9). In all this, he is faithfully reflecting his own Scriptures where sexual desire and its expression are a good and natural part of what it means to be human and a very particular way in which human companionship is offered, nurtured and sustained. To live within a sexually expressed, committed relationship is 'typical' in creation. It is a gift of God. To speak as if this desire, unlike many others, can simply be controlled and denied expression by simple choice or act of will would simply be a contradiction.

Paul leaves the choice of sexual abstinence or marriage to Christians themselves. He is wholly merciful, permission-giving and non-judgmental in this provision. So marriage or sexual abstinence is chosen by one who has 'determined in his own mind' (1 Corinthians 7.37). It is a personal matter. It is not imposed. That means there is no scriptural warrant for a community imposing celibacy on any of its members. It is a gift that can be freely chosen only by those who find the grace and resources to do so.

So how might this passage apply to those in the Christian community, living in readiness for the coming kingdom, who are gay? If it is not good to be alone, what of those for whom heterosexual marriage is not an option? What basis is found here for requiring lives of lifelong sexual abstinence from those who are clear that they do not have the gift of celibacy, whose 'passions are strong' (1 Corinthians 7.36), who lack the necessary 'control' needed to remain outside a sexual relationship but whose natural desire is for the companionship of someone of the same sex? What are they to do? Is it really better for them to be on fire than to marry? Nowhere here is celibacy imposed as a 'remedy' for supposedly *dis*ordered desires.

Christians who are gay and partnered are often accused by those who disagree with them of having made the easier choice – of choosing according to their own desires rather than submitting to the Bible or to God's will for them. I have to say, that is not my pastoral experience. Two people come to mind whom I have journeyed with in different times and places. Both had a passionate Christian faith formed in deeply Bible-centred churches. Both were painfully working through the fact that they were gay. Not unusually, neither of them felt that they could talk about this in their respective communities. One was a leader in a church where people regularly spoke in hostile terms about 'homosexuals'. One tried dating someone of the opposite sex but it simply confirmed where her own attractions lay. Both were deeply and utterly committed to obeying what they understood to be the teaching of Scripture. I watched and listened as they wrestled and agonized over this for an extended time. Neither showed any sign of having the charism of celibacy, though they had prayed hard for it. The struggle nearly broke both of them. If they had wanted an easier answer, they would have simply gone looking for a partner long ago. In her moving and often harrowing autobiography, Vicky Beeching describes her own similarly fierce and costly allegiance to the authority of Scripture, as interpreted within her Evangelical tradition, but that ultimately came at the price of her own mental and physical health.[3]

When God says, 'It is not good that the man should be alone' (Genesis 2.18), this is said of *all* human beings, not just heterosexual ones. So much of Paul's pastoral advice on choice, abstinence and 'not burning' speaks directly to the lives of gay men and women today. Some, like others in the Christian community, may choose singleness as a way of consecrated service in the kingdom, but for others, including faithful but harrowed Bible believers, might Paul not say, 'if his/her passions are strong, and so it has to be, let him/her marry . . . it is no sin'?

15

Sexuality and the sacred: joy, delight and sacrament

In the middle of the Bible is a short poem called 'The Song of Songs'. Its presence there continues to surprise. What is a celebration of erotic love and desire doing in the midst of the sacred texts of an ancient, conservative Near Eastern nation? Furthermore, in a world of patriarchal ordering, a love marked by joyful mutuality is told from the perspective of the woman and unfolds on her initiative. The couple are not married. It is startlingly public about sexual intimacies normally kept private. God is not mentioned at all. Nor are there any clear references to faith, prayer, worship or religious practice. This has led some to suggest that it is the least biblical book in the Bible. In fact, the Song is replete with poetic references to the Torah and the Temple and the language of the lovers is one of constant worship, petition and longing. The great first-century rabbi Akiva called this book 'the holiest of holies'. Professor Ellen Davis agrees and calls the Song the most biblical book of all.[1] In this sensual and highly allusive celebration of love and union, the whole Bible story is found.

The medieval Church delighted in this poem as a metaphor for contemplating the love between Christ and his bride, the Church. Long before that, it was speaking to the Jewish people of the devotion of Israel for the Torah: the Song is read aloud in synagogues during the Passover. Predictably, interest in the poem today tends to focus on human love and sex. Allegorical readings of mystical religious experience are likely to be mocked as attempts to avoid sex in a way all too typical of the Church down the centuries. As in all poetry, a variety of themes play at different levels and the imagery suggests multiple meanings. In this way, the Song holds together what is too often kept apart. The relationship of the spiritual and the sexual is wholly positive. Intimacy – human and sacred – are inseparably linked in this poem.

Davis suggests three ways in which this poem is relevant to today's world and the Church.[2] The Song celebrates 'the incomparable joy of faithful sexual relationship'. Without qualification or anxiety, it reveals the delights of committed desire and expression. The couple's freedom is exhilarating but neither casual nor indulgent: 'The Song is the strongest possible affirmation of the desire for intimate, harmonious, enduring relationships with the other.'[3]

The Song affirms that human intimacy finds its fullest meaning in the deeper intimacy and union with divine love. 'Genuine intimacy brings us into contact with the sacred', says Davis. Indeed, sexual love may well be the way some first come in touch with an ecstatic or spiritual dimension to life. This also means that 'our religious capacity is linked to an awareness of our own human sexuality'.[4]

The Song delights in 'the love of a beautiful land' – creation itself. Theologically the poem celebrates a reversal of all that was lost in the original garden in Genesis. All that was separated is now found restored. The couple embrace in unashamed delight in poetic imagery that, for those who recognize it, is constantly linked to Temple and divine worship. As this happens, all around them is bursting into pungent blossom, fruitfulness and exuberant growth. Indeed the sheer vibrancy of creation is a constant theme through the poem. When human desire and love find full expression the land itself returns to being the garden of God's gift, presence and delight. It is all mutual.

> My beloved speaks and says to me:
> 'Arise, my love, my fair one,
>   and come away;
> for now the winter is past,
>   the rain is over and gone.
> The flowers appear on the earth;
>   the time of singing has come . . .
> The fig tree puts forth its figs,
>   and the vines are in blossom;
>   they give forth fragrance.'
> (Song of Songs 2.10–13)

Throughout history the Christian faith has found the relationship between sexuality and spirituality very difficult. Sexual passion and holy living are not usually thought of as partners in Christian discipleship. The one is usually considered an obstacle to the other. The most common way the Church has tried to cope with this has been to keep the sexual and the spiritual firmly separate. The saints were those who had somehow transcended earthly passions and energies. Holiness was next to bodilessness and was most surely achieved by renouncing the earthly life. The poet Thomas James speaks memorably of learning to put on camouflage when going to church – covering himself 'with the body of a saint'.[5]

The cost of such a strategy is high, for what is being denied lies at the heart of being human and alive. When we start from a suspicion of embodied living we will always be seeking to tame or to separate ourselves from what is most primal, passionate and powerful within us. That means we will be cutting ourselves off from our deepest source of God-given creative energy. 'There is, in passion, a power that holiness needs.'[6]

Rather, our vocation is to be makers of love. That means learning how to faithfully and creatively indwell the calling to be human and sexual *without fear*. This does not require us to be in active sexual relationships. 'We do not need to be leading actively genital lives to come into contact with God's passionate love. But we do need to be in touch with the intensity and power of that force within us, for it is the same drive that leads both to God and toward another human person.'[7] Our sexual, erotic energies awaken in us far more than passing moments of physical or emotional satisfaction. There is a passion to be fully engaged, a search for a deeper unity of being and of belonging. We also meet it in our capacity for sublime creativity, our sensitivity to beauty and pain, our desire to reach out into the lives of others, our shared search for wholeness, meaning and purpose. Nothing is so ordinary and so transcendent, so empowering and so utterly disarming.

Given the limitless capacity of sexual desire to cause havoc and division, we might ask why God made it such a core part of the humanity he created in the beginning. Doesn't it continue to be more trouble than it is worth? What we do not have is the option of giving this back. Nor is there an 'off' switch. There is no 'safe' living on offer.

Perhaps it is our thorn in the flesh – an unsought (even unwanted) gift, to keep us humble and to teach us to live by the grace that is sufficient for our needs? Angela Tilby expresses something similar when she writes:

Our sexuality is the playground for prayer. It is where we tumble over our greatest needs and hungers, where the possibility of erotic delight is revealed, the limitations of self-love are exposed, and pride is purged . . . our sexuality remains the place of great personal intensity where we have the capacity to be most open and most closed to God because it remains a place of trouble and torment and also of the greatest earthly blessing and happiness.[8]

So perhaps one of the important gifts of our sexuality to our spiritual pilgrimage is to keep it all down to earth. It may embarrass us, distract us and confuse us, but the sheer messy earthiness of our sexual passions and energies keeps us praying and seeking God out of real, embodied human living. Christian spirituality involves *taking* flesh, not escaping from or abandoning it.

We are seeking a Christian vision for our humanity in the midst of a society that reflects deep confusion in the area of sexuality and relationships and that has abandoned Christian moral teaching and lifestyle. Exploited carelessly for pleasure, fearfully held at a distance or burdened with impossible expectations of fulfilment in relationships, human sexuality is the place where some of the deepest wounding and confusion in our culture are found.

The Church itself remains strongly conflicted regarding its response to this issue. All too often its response has been one familiarly found in anxious communities. Certain groups, beliefs or behaviours are identified as 'the problem'. These are then firmly expelled – and it works. Anxieties are eased – for a time. The tensions are eased, for a time. The process is not always conscious, but excluding cannot heal. Rather than separating, we must learn to listen. Richard Rohr writes:

Those at the edge of any system and those excluded from any system, ironically and invariably hold the secret for the conversion and wholeness of that very group. They always hold the feared, rejected, and denied parts of the group's soul.[9]

Recent autobiographies by Christian women and men who are gay reveal just how damaging it can be when such an innately human vocation is denied, repressed or judged as wrong in the Church and society (examples include Marcus Green, Stanley Underhill, Vicky Beeching, Jayne Ozanne and Nadia Bolz-Weber[10]).

In *Coming Out in the Black Country* (2018), a retired priest, Stanley Underhill, tells of his experience as a gay man in a church and society where such things could not be openly talked about and were kept hidden. An attempted exorcism and conversion therapies failed to 'cure' Underhill's desires. The relentless message was that there was something wrong with him. The therapies resulted in lifelong depression. 'Having had sex as a battleground throughout your life,' he says, 'you've missed out on any experience of intimacy, and the sacramental element of the union of two souls.' 'Love', says his interviewer. 'Love', says Underhill, 'I'm alone and I long for, I suppose, an experience of feeling one with another.'[11]

When the 'good' search for love, belonging and intimacy is happening in a society without moral compass, and where familiar boundaries for human relating have all but collapsed, it will often be a place of great wounding, hurt and bewilderment. The journey towards intimacy of any kind may be very difficult one. I have long valued the prayers of Jim Cotter. Among his many gifts he was a pastoral presence to many in the gay community wounded by both the sexual excesses and the judg-mental exclusions in our world. Cotter gave special attention to those most damaged through their search for love and sexual intimacy. For some, it was the result of their own compulsive confusions. For others, the wounds were inflicted by others – 'eunuchs who have been made eunuchs by others' (to adapt Jesus' words in Matthew 19.12). Cotter understood the journey of healing for many that this required, and was a wise guide:

When we come to the place of our wounded sexuality, healing cannot start from the place of passion . . . The temptation is to cut off from the ache of the wound and search desperately for sensation . . . Rather must the search be for other moments of bodily loving and touch, assured of another's steady love . . . small healing sacraments of touch, where loneliness is relieved, where delight is shared, where flesh is comforted, where sleep may come in another's arms . . . Only then, bodies deeply affirmed as good, can mightier moments of passion be contained . . .' And where the wounding is too deep, we have to be loyal to these other ways, and when we are, just as much love is made.[12]

I think it reveals much that we seem to lack a word in these discussions. It is a positive word that we need, somewhere be-tween 'promiscuous' and 'chaste'. A word that expresses a wholly celebratory, grateful way of actively indwelling this costly, joyful and holy vocation to be human and sexual:

God has created you a sexual being. God is at the heart of your striving, still creating you, always pursuing, luring, drawing, never letting go . . . Whatever your unique mix and measure of sexuality, be very glad: to be a human sexual is fundamental and ordinary and exceptional.[13]

The good news, in the midst of a society characterized by such casual, broken, misguided and destructive approaches to relationships, is that there are Christian couples who wish to make a public consecration of their love and commitment to one another before God and the world. Is this not something to celebrate? But this is precisely where the Church is most dead-locked and, perversely, where it withholds the blessing of God.

The Song does not have a romantic 'happy ending' either. The themes of losing and finding, joy and despair, continue, for such are the ways of love. This is our song too and we must learn to sing it in our times. We must re-learn what has too long been forgotten. Simply because they have had to seek this with such care, and at such personal cost and pain, I often hear the song more clearly sung by gay voices. In the midst of a heated online discussion, one such voice steadily affirmed what she knows from experience:

I believe lesbian and gay sexuality is loved and blessed by God, when it is an intimate and physical expression of tenderness, givenness, fidelity, care, joy, sharing, sacrifice, love. Sexuality is an integral part of being a human being, and a blessing of joy given to us; an expression of care and protection and love; a part of our wholeness; a part of how we can grow as people; a part of our healing. It is wonderful – whatever our genders.[14]

Love means love.

O God, Giver of life, Bearer of pain, Maker of love,
affirming in your incarnation the goodness of the flesh.
May the yearnings of our bodies
be fulfilled in sacraments of love
and our earthly embracings
a foretaste of the glory that shall be
in the light of the Resurrection of Jesus Christ.
Amen.[15]

Notes

1 On opening doors

1 Social opinion research supports this view. See Savi Hensman, 'Few British Christians think same-sex relationships "always wrong"', available online at: www.ekklesia.co.uk/node/24117, and Jayne Ozanne, 'Same-sex marriage: 2016 YouGov Poll', available online at: https://jayneozanne.com/2017/09/12/attitudes-to-same-sex-marriage-yougov-poll. See also Caroline Starkey and Grace Davie, 'Silence and words: Unexpected responses to a gay bishop', available online at: https://blogs.lse.ac.uk/religionglobalsociety/2019/12/silence-and-words-unexpected-responses-to-a-gay-bishop, which researches the huge number of supportive letters received following the public announcement by the Bishop of Grantham that he is gay and in a same-sex partnership – the first bishop in the Church of England to do so.

2 An initiative called Shared Conversations has already been running in the Church of England. It is based on the conviction that 'the subject of sexuality, with its history of deeply entrenched views, would be best addressed by facilitated conversations or a similar process to which the Church of England needs to commit itself at national and diocesan level' (www.sharedconversations.org).

3 Brownson, *Bible, Gender, Sexuality*, p. 12.

4 Martha Linden, 'Archbishop Justin Welby speaks out on gay relationships as he agrees to meet campaigner Peter Tatchell', *The Independent* (21 March 2013), available online at: www.

independent.co.uk/news/uk/home-news/archbishop-justin-welby-speaks-out-on-gay-relationships-as-he-agrees-to-meet-campaigner-peter-8543354.html.
5 Tolkien, *The Lord of the Rings*, pp. 322–6.

2 'That my house may be filled'

1 Chris Marshall, 'Kosher Christianity', graduation address at the Australian College of Theology, Auckland, New Zealand, 31 March 1990, p. 6 (unpublished).
2 Marshall, 'Kosher Christianity', p. 9.
3 Donovan, *Christianity Rediscovered*, p. xix (my emphasis).

3 The surprise of God?

1 Tomkins, *Journey to the Mayflower*, p. 330. Robinson's words also inspired the hymn 'We limit not the truth of God', available online at: https://hymnary.org/text/we_limit_not_the_truth_of_God.
2 O'Donovan, '"One man and one woman"'. The surprise is also where this quotation is found. This thoughtful collection of essays comes from a group of biblically conservative theologians.
3 Kuhn, *Having Words with God*, p. 89 (my emphasis).
4 Kuhn, *Having Words with God*, pp. 8–10. For a more detailed example, see Kenneth Bailey's analysis of Jesus' use of Old Testament texts in his Nazareth sermon (Luke chapter 4) in *Jesus through Middle Eastern Eyes*, Chapter 12.
5 Kuhn, *Having Words with God*, p. 16.
6 N. T. Wright, 'How can the Bible be authoritative?' (12 July 2016), available online at: http://ntwrightpage.com/2016/07/12/how-can-the-Bible-be-authoritative.
7 See Alexander, *Creation or Evolution*, pp. 139–41.
8 Marshall, *Beyond the Bible*, p. 78.

9 The Virginia Report (Inter-Anglican Theological and Doctrinal Commission), cited in Groves (ed.), *The Anglican Communion and Homosexuality*, p. 84.

4 The Bible in an age of anxiety

1 The national charity Anxiety UK (www.anxietyuk.org.uk) provides resources for those affected by anxiety disorders.
2 Friedman, *Failure of Nerve*, pp. 58–9.
3 http://merriam-webster.com/dictionary/anxiety.
4 Jantz, *Overcoming Anxiety, Worry, and Fear*, p. 420.
5 Stead, *Mindfulness and Christian Spirituality*, p. 6.
6 House of Bishops, 'Report of the House of Bishops Working Group on Human Sexuality'.
7 Church of England, 'Pilling Report published' (28 November 2013), available online at: www.churchofengland.org/more/media-centre/news/pilling-report-published.

5 Reading the Bible with Jesus

1 Bailey, *Jesus through Middle Eastern Eyes*, p. 297.
2 Wright, 'How can the Bible be authoritative?'
3 Bebbington, *Evangelicalism in Modern Britain*, p. 57.
4 Wright, 'How can the Bible be authoritative?'
5 Stott, *Baptism and Fullness*, p. 15.
6 Pennington, *Reading the Gospels Wisely*, p. 231.
7 Church of England, Mission Theological Advisory Group, *Presence and Prophecy*, pp. ix; see also p. 58.
8 Ford, *Christian Wisdom*, pp. 55, 295.

6 'Lie the lyings of a woman'

1 Translation by Dr John Bimson, Old Testament scholar and former faculty colleague, with grateful thanks.

2 Lings, *Love Lost in Translation*, p. 228.

3 Hartley, *Leviticus*, p. 297.

4 Gagnon, *The Bible and Homosexual Practice*, p. 56.

5 This argument is detailed in Walsh, 'Leviticus 18:22 and 20:13', p. 205.

6 Gagnon, *The Bible and Homosexual Practice*, p. 75.

7 Brownson, *Bible, Gender, Sexuality*, p. 269.

8 Keen, *Scripture, Ethics, and the Possibility of Same-Sex Relationships*, p. 51.

9 Keen helpfully illustrates this from the law requiring a rapist to marry his victim (Deuteronomy 22.28–29). To modern ears, this law simply compounds the original abuse, but she points out that the law is concerned with two things: it makes the rapist accountable and it is concerned with the well-being and care of the woman. In that society, a woman who had lost her virginity would be unable to marry and so would face lifelong hardship and destitution. The intent of that law was therefore to provide for the care and future of the victim. Keen writes, 'Today, we still strive to hold rapists accountable and protect women's wellbeing. But we do so in alternative ways that actually *enhance* that intent. We have imagined possibilities for better supporting women in that situation' (*Scripture, Ethics, and the Possibility of Same-Sex Relationships*, p. 52).

10 Keen, *Scripture, Ethics, and the Possibility of Same-Sex Relationships*, p. 52.

11 Lings, *Love Lost in Translation*, p. 228.

12 From the conclusion of the discussion by Ian Paul on 'Leviticus and same-sex relations', Psephizo, available online at: www.psephizo.com/biblical-studies/leviticus-and-same-sex-relations.

7 Romans and the wrath of God

1 Nazarite vows in the Old Testament specifically forbade the cutting of a man's hair. Paul could not be contradicting his own Scriptures (Numbers 6.1–21).

2 James Alison, 'But the Bible says? A Catholic reading of Romans' (12 January 2004), available online at: www.jamesalison.co.uk/texts/eng15.html.

3 Athenagoras, Apology 34, cited by Jonathan Tallon, 'Does the Bible really say . . . anything at all about homosexuality as we understand it today?' (17 May 2019), available online at: https://viamedia.news/2019/05/17/does-the-Bible-really-say-anything-at-all-about-homosexuality-as-we-understand-it-today.

4 In what follows, I acknowledge my debt to an unpublished paper by Bishop David Atkinson.

5 Moore, *A Question of Truth*, p. 104.

8 On giving it a name

1 The one exception is a letter in the archive from a theological student challenging the appropriateness of the word 'homosexual' to translate *arsenokoitai*. There is no record of any reply (Kathy Baldock, 'How and when the word homosexual was first introduced into the Bible' (25 November 2017), available online at: http://canyonwalkerconnections.com/word-homosexual-first-introduced-Bible).

9 The sin of Sodom

1 Lings, *Love Lost in Translation*, p. 241.

2 Alison, *Faith beyond Resentment*, p. 45.

10 'Male and female he created them'

1 For evidence of the continuing tendency in today's world, see Criado Perez, *Invisible Women*, p. 3.
2 I refer to the six texts traditionally assumed to refer to homosexuality and same-sex relationships: Genesis 19.1–9; Leviticus 18.22; 20.13; Romans 1.24–27; 1 Corinthians 6.9; 1 Timothy 1.10.
3 Plato, *Symposium*, 192a–d.
4 Gagnon, *The Bible and Homosexual Practice*, pp. 485, 487–88.
5 Gagnon, *The Bible and Homosexual Practice*, p. 488.
6 See Brownson's critique of this view in *Bible, Gender, Sexuality*, pp. 26–9.
7 Williams, *Roman Homosexuality*, p. 3.
8 Moore, *A Question of Truth*, p. 111.
9 Summary of 100 surveys in Compton, 'Kids can thrive with gay parents'. See also Hagger-Holt and Hagger-Holt, *Pride and Joy*.
10 'Statement from the Archbishop of Canterbury following today's General Synod' (15 February 2017), available online at: www.archbishopofcanterbury.org/speaking-and-writing/speeches/statement-archbishop-canterbury-following-todays-general-synod.

11 One flesh

1 Complementarianism is the view that men and women have different but complementary roles and responsibilities in marriage, family life, religious leadership and elsewhere. The conservative Evangelical tradition teaches the permanent subordination of women to men, on the basis that this reflects a permanent subordination of the Son to the Father in the life of the Trinity. Subordinationism was a belief the Church

wrestled with and came to reject through its opposition to the Arian heresy in the fourth century. It is not supported in the historic creeds and confessions of faith.

2 Josiah Idowu-Fearon, 'The global excitement about Lambeth Conference', Anglican Communion News Service (15 February 2019), available online at: www.anglicannews. org/blogs/2019/02/the-global-excitement-about-lambeth-conference.aspx. The Lambeth Conference is a gathering of all the bishops in the worldwide Anglican Communion. It is held in Canterbury every ten years.

3 Brownson, *Bible, Gender, Sexuality*, p. 34.

4 Brownson, *Bible, Gender, Sexuality*, p. 87.

5 Davis, *Proverbs, Ecclesiastes, and the Song of Songs*, pp. 150–1.

6 Moore, *A Question of Truth*, p. 147.

7 See Meg Warner's critique of this claim in 'Elephants, penguins, procreation & Japanese knotweed', ViaMedia. News (8 February 2019), available online at: https://viamedia. news/2019/02/08/elephants-penguins-procreation-japanese-knotweed.

8 These words remain in a revised form of the marriage service still being commended by the Church of England as 'ideal for couples seeking a traditional language ceremony' (*Common Worship: Alternative services. Series one: Solemnization of matrimony*, London: Church House, 2005).

9 O'Donovan, *Church in Crisis*, pp. 114–15.

10 Taylor, 'An invitation to the feast'.

11 Song, *Covenant and Calling*.

12 Call nothing unclean

1 Alison, 'Towards global inclusion of LGBT people within Catholic communities'.

13　Good fruit

1 'Justin Welby speaks of same-sex challenges for Church', BBC News (21 March 2013), available online at: www.bbc.co.uk/news/uk-21860447.

2 I have reported nothing here of this sensitive story that is not in the public domain, for example, 'Didsbury church's radical change after gay girl's suicide', BBC News, available online at: www.bbc.co.uk/news/av/uk-england-manchester-45615029/didsbury-church-s-radical-change-after-gay-girl-s-suicide.

3 The church's policy of inclusivity is outlined at https://stjamesandemmanuel.org/inclusion.

4 'Letter from the Archbishops of Canterbury and York following General Synod', The Church of England (February 2017), available online at: www.churchofengland.org/more/media-centre/news/letter-archbishops-canterbury-and-york-following-general-synod.

5 Steven Croft, 'Clothe yourselves with love', Bishop Steven's blog, available online at: https://blogs.oxford.anglican.org/clothe-yourselves-with-love.

6 An unnamed contributor on a social media discussion thread.

14　To whom it is given

1 Goergen, *The Sexual Celibate*, p. 39.

2 Moore, *A Question of Truth*, p. 100.

3 Beeching, *Undivided*.

15　Sexuality and the sacred

1 Davis, *Proverbs, Ecclesiastes, and the Song of Songs*, p. 231.

2 Davis, *Proverbs, Ecclesiastes, and the Song of Songs*, pp. 233–7.

3 Davis, *Proverbs, Ecclesiastes, and the Song of Songs*, p. 235.

4 Davis, *Proverbs, Ecclesiastes, and the Song of Songs*, p. 235.

5 James, *Letters to a Stranger*.
6 Lavelle, *The Meaning of Holiness*, p. 40.
7 Carroll and Dyckman, *Chaos or Creation*, pp. 128–9.
8 Tilby, 'Prayer and sexuality', pp. 94–95.
9 Richard Rohr, adapted from *Radical Grace*, 28, day 2.
10 See Bibliography for details.
11 'Marcus Green and Stanley Underhill, two gay priests of different generations, in conversation', *Church Times* (15 February 2019), available online at: www.churchtimes.co.uk/articles/2019/15-february/regulars/podcast/podcast-marcus-green-and-stanley-underhill-two-gay-priests-of-different-generations-in-conversation.
12 Prayer 'O God, Giver of life, Bearer of pain . . .', pp. 75-6, by Jim Cotter from *Prayer at Night* © Jim Cotter 1989. Published by Cairns Press. Used by permission. rights@hymnsam.co.uk
13 Cotter, *Prayer at Night*, p. 76.
14 Susannah, a contributor to an online discussion on a social media thread.
15 Cotter, *Prayer at Night*, p. 76.

Bibliography and further reading

Alexander, Denis, *Creation or Evolution*. Oxford: Monarch, 2008.

Alison, James, *Faith beyond Resentment: Fragments Catholic and gay*. London: DLT, 1997.

Alison, James, 'Towards global inclusion of LGBT people within Catholic communities: A new theological approach', *America: The Jesuit Review* (2 October, 2014), available online at: www.americamagazine.org/issue/towards-global-inclusion-lgbt-people-within-catholic-communities.

Bailey, Kenneth, *Jesus through Middle Eastern Eyes: Cultural studies in the Gospels*. London: SPCK, 2008.

Bebbington, David, *Evangelicalism in Modern Britain: A history from the 1730s to the 1980s*. Abingdon: Routledge, 1988.

Beeching, Vicky, *Undivided: Coming out, becoming whole, and living free from shame*. London: Collins, 2018.

Bolz-Weber, Nadia, *Shameless: A sexual revolution*. Norwich: Canterbury Press, 2019.

Brownson, James, *Bible, Gender, Sexuality*. Grand Rapids, MI: Eerdmans, 2013.

Bryan, Christopher, *And God Spoke: The authority of the Bible in the Church today*. Cambridge, MA: Cowley Publications, 2002.

Burridge, Richard, *Imitating Jesus: An inclusive approach to New Testament ethics*. Grand Rapids, MI: Eerdmans, 2007.

Carroll, L. Patrick, and Katherine Marie Dyckman, *Chaos or Creation: Spirituality in mid-life*. Mahwah, NJ: Paulist Press, 1986.

Church of England, Mission Theological Advisory Group, *Presence and Prophecy: A heart for mission in theological education*. London: Church House Publishing, 2002.

Compton, Rebecca, 'Kids can thrive with gay parents', *Psychology Today* (21 November 2016), available online at: www.psychologytoday.com/us/blog/adopting-reason/201611/kids-can-thrive-gay-parents.

Cotter, Jim, *Prayer at Night*. Norwich: Cairns Press, 1989.

Criado Perez, Caroline, *Invisible Women: Data bias in a world designed for men*. London: Chatto & Windus, 2019.

Davis, Ellen F., *Proverbs, Ecclesiastes, and the Song of Songs*. Louisville, KY: Westminster John Knox Press, 2004.

Donovan, Vincent J., *Christianity Rediscovered*. London: SCM Press, 2001.

Ecclestone, Alan, *Yes to God*. London: DLT, 1990.

Ford, David, *Christian Wisdom: Desiring God and learning in love*. Cambridge: Cambridge University Press, 2007.

Friedman, Edwin H., *A Failure of Nerve: Leadership in the age of the quick fix*. New York: Seabury, 2007.

Gagnon, Robert A. J., *The Bible and Homosexual Practice: Texts and hermeneutics*. Nashville, TN: Abingdon Press, 2001.

Goergen, Donald, *The Sexual Celibate*. New York: Seabury, 1979.

Gordan, Joseph K., *Scripture in History: A systematic theology of the Christian Bible*. Notre Dame, IN: University of Notre Dame Press, 2019.

Green, Marcus, *The Possibility of Difference*. Stowmarket: Kevin Mayhew, 2018.

Groves, Philip (ed.), *The Anglican Communion and Homosexuality*. London: SPCK, 2008.

Hagger-Holt, Sarah, and Rachel Hagger-Holt, *Pride and Joy: A guide for lesbian, gay, bisexual and trans parents*. London: Pinter & Martin, 2017.

Hartley, John E., *Leviticus*, vol. 4 of *Word Biblical Commentary*. Grand Rapids, MI: Zondervan, 1992.

House of Bishops, 'Report of the House of Bishops Working Group on Human Sexuality'. London: Church House Publishing, 2013, available online at: www.churchofengland.org/sites/default/files/2018-01/GS%201929%20Working%20Group%20on%20human%20sexuality_0.pdf.

James, Thomas, *Letters to a Stranger*. Minneapolis, MN: Graywolf Press, 2008.

Jantz, Gregory. *Overcoming Anxiety, Worry, and Fear: Practical ways to find peace*. Grand Rapids, MI: Revell, 2011.

Keen, Karen R., *Scripture, Ethics, and the Possibility of Same-Sex Relationships*. Grand Rapids, MI: Eerdmans, 2018.

Kuhn, Karl Allen, *Having Words with God: The Bible as conversation*. Minneapolis, MN: Fortress Press, 2008.

Lavelle, Louis, *The Meaning of Holiness*. London: Burns & Oates, 1951.

Lings, K. Renato, *Love Lost in Translation: Homosexuality and the Bible*. Bloomington, IN: Trafford Publishing, 2013.

Marshall, I. Howard, *Beyond the Bible: Moving from Scripture to theology*. Grand Rapids, MI: Baker Academic; Milton Keynes: Paternoster, 2004.

Moore, Gareth, *A Question of Truth*. London: Continuum, 2003.

Noble, Thomas A., Sarah K. Whittle and Philip S. Johnston (eds), *Marriage, Family and Relationships: Biblical, doctrinal and contemporary perspectives*. London: Apollos, 2017.

O'Donovan, Oliver, *Church in Crisis: The gay controversy and the Anglican Communion*. London: SCM Press, 2008.

Ozanne, Jayne, *Just Love: A journey of self-acceptance*. London: DLT, 2018.

Pennington, Jonathan T., *Reading the Gospels Wisely: A narrative and theological introduction*. Grand Rapids, MI: Baker Academic, 2012.

Rohr, Richard, *Radical Grace: Daily meditations*. Cincinnati, OH: St Anthony Messenger Press, 1993.

Song, Robert, *Covenant and Calling: Towards a theology of same-sex relationships*. London: SCM Press, 2013.

Stead, Tim, *Mindfulness and Christian Spirituality: Making space for God*. London: SPCK, 2016.

Stott, John, R. W., *Baptism and Fullness: The work of the Holy Spirit today*. London: IVP, 1975.

Taylor, Simon, 'An invitation to the feast: A positive biblical approach to equal marriage', *Modern Believing*, 58: 1 (January, 2017), available online at: www.cofe-equal-marriage.org.uk/wp-content/uploads/resources/an-invitation-to-the-feast-a-positive-biblical-approach-to-equal-marriage.pdf.

Tilby, Angela, 'Prayer and sexuality', in Fraser N. Watts (ed.), *Perspectives on Prayer*. London: SPCK, 2002.

Tolkien, J. R. R., *The Lord of the Rings*. London: Allen & Unwin, 1966.

Tomkins, Stephen, *The Journey to the Mayflower: God's outlaws and the invention of freedom*. London: Hodder & Stoughton, 2020.

Underhill, Stanley, *Coming Out in the Black Country*, London: Zuleika, 2018.

Walsh, J. T., 'Leviticus 18:22 and 20:13: Who is doing what to whom?', *Journal of Biblical Literature*, 120: 2 (2001), 201–9, available online at: http://web.archive.org/web/20070104151350/http://www.sbl-site.org/Publications/JBL/JBL1202.pdf.

Williams, Craig A., *Roman Homosexuality*. Oxford: Oxford University Press, 2010.

WE HAVE A VISION OF A WORLD IN WHICH EVERYONE IS TRANSFORMED BY CHRISTIAN KNOWLEDGE

As well as being an award-winning publisher, SPCK is the oldest Anglican mission agency in the world.

Our mission is to lead the way in creating books and resources that help everyone to make sense of faith.

Will you partner with us to put good books into the hands of prisoners, great assemblies in front of schoolchildren and reach out to people who have not yet been transformed by the Christian faith?

To donate, please visit www.spckpublishing.co.uk/donate or call our friendly fundraising team on 020 7592 3900.